S0-BFC-830

PG
3337
.G6
01336
1998

Goncharov's Oblomov.

GON

$17.95

DATE			
	WITHDRAWN		

BAKER & TAYLOR

61821

GONCHAROV'S *OBLOMOV*

A Critical Companion

Edited by Galya Diment

Northwestern University Press

The American Association of Teachers of

Slavic and East European Languages

Northwestern University Press

Evanston, Illinois 60208-4210

Copyright © 1998 by Northwestern University Press. Published 1998.

All rights reserved.

Printed in the United States of America

ISBN 0-8101-1405-4

Library of Congress Cataloging-in-Publication Data

Goncharov's Oblomov : a critical companion / edited by Galya

Diment.

     p. cm. — (Northwestern/AATSEEL critical companions

to Russian literature)

Includes bibliographical references.

ISBN 0-8101-1405-4 (paper : alk. paper)

   1. Goncharov, Ivan Aleksandrovich, 1812–1891. Oblomov.

I. Diment, Galya. II. Series.

PG3337.G6I1336 1998

891.73'3—dc21   97-50518

                                 CIP

The paper used in this publication meets the minimum requirements of the American National Standard for Information Sciences—Permanence of Paper for Printed Library Materials, ANSI Z39.48-1984.

Contents

Acknowledgments

All the articles and translations appearing here have been solicited specially for this volume. My initial editorial intent was to mix old and new, and include some of the best of the previous criticism on *Oblomov*, such as Dobrolyubov's pioneering "What's Oblomovitis?," Leon Stillman's excellent essay "Oblomovka Revisited," and Milton Ehre's discussion of *Oblomov* in his seminal English-language study of Goncharov. Yet, as I embarked on working on the companion more closely, I began to feel that there was so much that was still unsaid about this fascinating novel, and so many of Goncharov's autobiographical materials and relevant early writings which were still untranslated that, given the limited space, reprinting essays which are readily available in other publications was not the most judicious use of resources. I would, however, like to acknowledge our indebtedness to other Goncharov scholars whose works, while not included, are discussed and quoted here, and, in particular, to Milton Ehre, whose *Oblomov and His Creator* is easily the most cited study in this volume.

I would also like to thank Barry Scherr, the founding editor of the series, who first approached me about undertaking this project; Susan Harris, the very professional, enthusiastic, and friendly editor-in-chief at Northwestern University Press; and Ellen R. Feldman, managing editor at the Press, who oversaw the publication of the manuscript with care, attention to details, and graceful tact. I am also immensely grateful to all the contributors, who, in addition to enriching this volume with excellent articles and translations, were disciplined, punctual, and made my work as editor extremely easy and rewarding.

A Note on Transliteration

Consistent transliteration was particularly hard in this volume since we had to be constantly aware of the way the names of Goncharov's characters appear in various English translations. We chose to feature them the way they appear in David Magarshack's translation of the novel, which is the one most often used. We also rendered Russian first names in their more common Anglicized form – e.g., Andrey, Nikolay, Avdotya. Likewise, we used the more familiar spellings of famous last names – Tolstoy, Dostoevsky, Polevoy, etc. For the rest, we generally followed the more accurate Library of Congress system of transliteration. Now and then this strategy created odd instances – as when the patronymic of Oblomov's landlady and subsequent wife is spelled, as in Magarshack, "Matveyevna," while Goncharov's mother, who has the same patronymic, is referred to as "Matveevna," in accordance with the Library of Congress system. Other examples include "Alexeev," as a character in the novel, and "Alekseev," as an author whose works on Goncharov are cited in the volume. Such oddities were, however, virtually impossible to avoid once it became necessary to use different transliteration systems.

I   INTRODUCTION

The Precocious Talent
of Ivan Goncharov

GALYA DIMENT

Serene and steady, slightly ironic, moderately Epicurean, witty and kind, Goncharov, this Volga-region Horace, is accessible to all.
Yuly Aikhenvald

No other novel has been used to describe the ever-so-elusive "Russian mentality" or "Russian soul" as frequently as *Oblomov* by Ivan Goncharov, published in 1859. This is quite an achievement for a book in which the main protagonist spends most of his time asleep, thus mocking the very notions of plot, suspense, and character development that were the cornerstones of many other nineteenth-century Russian and European novels.

Despite being among the most popular novels in all of Russian literature, *Oblomov* has somehow failed to give its creator the status of a truly "major" Russian author. Instead, Goncharov is often delegated to a large and rather bland group of the so-called minor Russian realists. Typical in this respect is a remark by Vladimir Nabokov who, in *Speak, Memory*, lumps Goncharov with writers such as Grigorovich, Korolenko, and Mamin-Sibiriak, calling them all "stupefying bores . . . comparable to American 'regional writers.'"[1] And yet as a literary talent Goncharov was definitely no Oblomov-like slouch. To the contrary, he was both precocious and original: his unusual characters, themes, and surprisingly innovative literary techniques often anticipate groundbreaking writers to come, among them Chekhov, who wrote once that Goncharov was "10 heads above me in talent,"[2] and even Samuel Beckett, who read and greatly admired *Oblomov*.

What accounts, then, for this general critical underestimation of Ivan Goncharov as a writer? Some of it probably has to do with how Goncharov's literary contemporaries viewed him. He was the son of a merchant at a time when merchants were still derided in literature rather than encouraged to write it.[3] When already a published author, he chose to remain a government official while government officials were, often legitimately, seen as antithetical rather than conducive to literature's development. Insecure, reserved, and uncomfortable at large gatherings, he was deemed cold, secretive, and egotistical. Slavophiles resented him for making a Russian character in *Oblomov* lazy and apathetic, while bestowing his German Stolz with numerous virtues.[4] Liberals, on the other hand, strongly objected to his service as a government censor under a very conservative tsar and could not forgive him what they deemed were "reactionary" tendencies in his last published novel, *The Precipice*. A highly publicized literary squabble with Ivan Turgenev, during which Goncharov accused Turgenev of stealing ideas from him, also did not improve Goncharov's reputation.[5]

Consequently, Goncharov's fellow writers were often truly devastating in their comments. Even before their public debacle, Turgenev apparently complained to his friends that Goncharov had "the soul of a bureaucrat, a world view limited to most petty interests, [and] a nature that knows no spiritual impulses." He also wrongly predicted that Goncharov would never write more than one novel.[6] Dostoevsky's verdict was almost identical. Goncharov, he wrote in 1856, "possesses the soul of a bureaucrat, no ideas, and the eyes of a boiled fish."[7] The admirers of Goncharov's talent were hardly more sparing. Vissarion Belinsky, the most influential Russian critic at the time, was very enthusiastic about Goncharov's first novel, *A Common Story*, and instrumental in its publication, but he still referred to its author as "a petty and repulsive individual."[8] Chekhov, likewise, tempered his high praise for Goncharov's talent with the phrase, "though I don't like him as a person."[9]

Many of these negative assessments of Goncharov appear to have been largely undeserved. He was a careful man who did not want to jeopardize his government career, but he was in many ways among the most progressive of Russia's intelligentsia. Like Petr Aduev in *A Common Story*, Goncharov was an Anglophile, yet on visiting the English colonies in Africa and Asia in the 1850s, he was genuinely disturbed by the fate of the colonialized peoples, finding the treatment of them by the English "animal-like, . . . rude, cold, and full of contempt."[10] While in Siberia, he frequently visited the exiled Decembrists remaining in Irkutsk, even though they were yet to be pardoned by the tsar whom he served. As Beth Holmgren remarks in her article for this volume, Goncharov was also unusually sympathetic to the problems that smart and capable women – like Lizaveta Aleksandrovna in *A Common Story* or Olga Ilyinskaya in *Oblomov* – experienced in a society that appeared to have little desire to accommodate them.

Goncharov's contemporaries, often favoring strong literary showings of an author's ideological or moral beliefs (the apparent lack of which endangered Pushkin's posthumous reputation as well), tended to misread not only Goncharov's personality but also his novels, overlooking their huge personal dimensions and reducing Goncharov's complex characters to simplistic types. Belinsky started this trend by discussing the Aduevs in *A Common Story* merely as representatives of the old and the new orders, of the fading romanticism and emerging realism, of provincial naïveté and urban sophisticated practicality. He also began a tradition of depicting Goncharov as a cold and impersonal observer who "has neither love nor hostility towards the characters he creates" and whose talent while "strong [and] remarkable" is not "major" (*ne pervostepennyi*).[11]

It is obviously too late – and hardly worth our while – to try to unravel in its entirety the convoluted web that affected Goncharov's relationships with his fellow writers and critics and ultimately damaged his reputation and literary stature. One thing is clear, though. Like no other Russian writer of the nineteenth century, Goncharov begs for – and deserves – rereading and reevaluation. And it is precisely because of the largely precocious nature of Goncharov's artistic temperament and talent that his best and most appreciative readers may be found not among *his* contemporaries but among *ours*.

Before *Oblomov*

The future creator of *Oblomov* was born in the Volga town of Simbirsk on June 6, 1812. His father was a wealthy merchant for whom a marriage to Ivan's mother, thirty years his junior and herself a daughter of a merchant, was his second. Fifty-eight years old at the time of his son's birth, Alexander Goncharov was to die seven years later, leaving his widow with four children, of whom the youngest was less than a year old.

Some critics talk of Oblomov as "a classical example of a man suffering from a severe mother complex,"[12] and whether or not we agree with this diagnosis, one thing is relatively clear: Avdotya Matveevna Goncharova (née Shakhtorina) was an overwhelming presence for Oblomov's creator. She was poorly educated but strong-willed and, according to her son, very intelligent. "Our mother was truly bright," Goncharov wrote to his brother Nikolay in 1862. "She was undoubtedly smarter than all the women I have known."[13] Upon his mother's demise in 1851, Goncharov wrote to his sister Alexandra: "I feel privileged and I praise God that I had such a mother. There is nothing and no one about whom my thoughts are so radiant and my memories so sacred as about her."[14]

When Goncharov's father died, he left his family well provided for. The household, according to Goncharov, was large and prosperous:

> The structures were numerous: serfs' living quarters, stables, cattle yards, sheds, barns, chicken coops, baths. We had our own horses, cows, even goats and sheep, chickens and ducks. . . . All our barns, store rooms, and ice cellars were stuffed with supplies of flour, grain, and all kinds of provisions needed for feeding us and our numerous domestic serfs. In short, a whole estate, a village.[15]

They also had a guest cottage that was inhabited by a tenant, Nikolay Tregubov, a former naval officer, who, while Alexander Goncharov was still alive, had become a close family friend and eventually the godfather to all the Goncharov children. It is quite likely that Alexander Goncharov, knowing he would probably die before his children reached maturity, had an unofficial agreement with Tregubov that the latter would step in and help the widow to raise and educate the children. Tregubov was rich, single, well-educated, and of noble birth. He was also a Freemason. (Simbirsk had one of the oldest and better-established Masonic lodges in the country.)[16]

Soon after Goncharov's father died, Tregubov moved into the main house and did indeed assume the role of a surrogate father. Since he was a bachelor, and since Avdotya Matveevna, still a relatively young and apparently attractive woman, never remarried, it is also quite possible that Tregubov became a surrogate husband as well (not unlike Oblomov in his relationship with Agafya Matveyevna[17] or Goncharov in his own liaison with a housekeeper, Alexandra Ivanovna Treigut, a widow and mother of three, for whose education and welfare Goncharov assumed full responsibility).[18] Goncharov described the arrangement between Tregubov and Avdotya Goncharova as follows:

> Upon our father's death . . . he moved from a cottage to the main house and occupied half of it. . . . Our mother, who was grateful to him for taking over the difficult responsibility for our education, took over herself all the obligations for the household and his physical existence. His serfs, cooks, grooms merged with ours and were placed under my mother's supervision – and we lived as one family. All material considerations fell on my mother, an excellent, experienced, and disciplined housekeeper. All intellectual concerns were his.[19]

Tregubov, although caring and well-meaning, apparently did not carry out his part of the bargain very well. Goncharov thought the early education he received under Tregubov's supervision was chaotic and haphazard. First the boy studied under the tutelage of a town woman, who, according to him, was "mean and used to hit students on their fingers with a belt if their handwriting was not neat."[20] An avid reader, Goncharov read all the books in his household by the time he was nine. He read them, he recalled later, "one after the other, at random, without anyone close by to share impressions or opinions about what I had read."[21] In 1820 Goncharov was placed in a more satisfactory boarding school, situated on the other side of the Volga, which was not unlike the school Andrey Stolz's father kept and Iliusha Oblomov attended. There he also obtained access to more books but soon exhausted that library as well.

"There was neither a library nor a theater in town," Goncharov was to complain later.[22] And, indeed, Simbirsk at the time was a far cry from a cultural Mecca. Deeply provincial and slow-paced, it struck visitors as one of the "quietest, sleepiest, and most stagnant" towns in all of Russia.[23] In 1836 Lermontov immortalized Simbirsk's proverbially indolent nature in one of his poems: "Sleep and laziness had overtaken Simbirsk. Even the Volga rolled here slower and smoother."[24] Goncharov's own descriptions of his birthplace were similar. "The whole appearance of my home town," he reminisced in 1887, "was a perfect picture of sleepiness and stagnation. . . . One wanted himself to fall asleep while looking at all this immobility, at sleepy windows with their curtains and blinds drawn, at sleepy faces one saw inside the houses or on streets. 'We have nothing to do!' – they seemed to be saying while yawning and lazily looking at you. 'We are in no hurry.'"[25]

When Goncharov was ten, his mother and Tregubov sent him to study in Moscow with his older brother, Nikolay, at the School of Commerce. It was probably only natural for Goncharov's mother and godfather to assume that this school, which enjoyed a fairly good reputation, should be a logical place for the ambitious sons of a merchant. Goncharov hated it, though. He stayed there eight years, four of which were spent in the same grade simply because he happened to be among the youngest students. He confessed to his brother later that it was too painful for him even to recall his time at the school: stupid, despotic, and frequently drunk teachers, excruciatingly boring class sessions, outdated textbooks, snail-like pace, no room for creativity or imagination. It was, Goncharov concluded, a total waste of the brothers' time and of their mother's money.[26]

Goncharov's School of Commerce experience appears to have been so traumatic, in fact, that it left deep emotional scars for the rest of his life. Although in his private thoughts he probably blamed Tregubov for having sent him to the wrong school (his uneducated mother, after all, did not know any better), in his correspondence with friends he tended to attribute the severe shortcomings of his early education mostly to his social origins. "Your advantages," he wrote to an aristocratic friend once, "consist of having had a systematic education. . . . If only you knew how much dirt, indecency, pettiness . . . I had to go through since birth. . . . What to others is given by nature and by their surroundings, I had to create in myself single-handedly, with laborious efforts. . . . And I did not even possess any natural resources on which to build since they all had been ruined by the lack of early, careful education."[27]

In June 1830 Goncharov returned to Simbirsk without having graduated from the School of Commerce. His mother cited financial difficulties as one of the reasons for taking her son out, but Goncharov's long-term unhappiness with the institution must have also finally registered with her. Two months later Goncharov was, much to his relief, "freed from the guild of merchants" by the Magistracy of the City of Simbirsk and thus achieved a right not to follow in his father's footsteps but "to enroll in a university and then pursue a government or academic career."[28]

From 1831 on, Goncharov's life followed a pattern typical of his generation of writers and men of letters, the first one not to be dominated by members of the Russian aristocracy. Having successfully passed the entrance exams, Goncharov entered the Department of Philology of Moscow University. The 1830s were one of the more dramatic periods in the history of Russian universities. On the one hand, the early reign of Nicholas I was already beginning to display its strongly paranoid tendencies, as when in 1834 government inspectors were planted in universities to watch over students' activities outside the classroom. On the other hand, Nicholas's government was also spending large sums of money for new university buildings, libraries, and laboratories, as well as increasing professorial salaries in order to attract the best specialists to teaching.[29] While at the university Goncharov studied under some of the most influential minds in the country and also met several important literary figures: Lermontov was a fellow student for a short while, and in 1832 Goncharov's idol, Pushkin, visited one of his classes.[30]

On graduating from Moscow University in 1835, Goncharov moved to St. Petersburg and began working as a translator in the Department of Foreign Trade of the Ministry of Finances. Life in the Russian capital at the time was picking up speed. Nicholas was busy creating new departments and ministries, of which the Department of Foreign Trade was one of the fastest growing since foreign trade was on a steep rise.[31] St. Petersburg was also rapidly becoming the "hub" of Russia's emerging market economy, which had spread to facilitate both the thriving trade and the ever-increasing populations of merchants, craftsmen, and other professionals. In Goncharov's *A Common Story* Petr Aduev is shown to be a co-owner of a privately owned factory, and such factories employing free, as opposed to serf, labor were indeed becoming commonplace.

These industrial, as well as rapid, scientific and technological advances appear to have contributed to the society's hardening spirit of pragmatism and utilitarianism, which was also palpable among Goncharov's contemporary Russian intelligentsia. It was quite a change for a generation raised on the literature and philosophy of Russian and West European idealism, romanticism, and sentimentalism, whose youthful sensibilities had been shaped by the likes of Byron, Schiller, or, closer to home, Nikolay Karamzin (Goncharov's own early favorite, who also hailed from Simbirsk). In a classical case of "fathers and sons," by the 1830s many of these intellectuals had turned against the idols of their youth. Most prominent in that group was Vissarion Belinsky, whose early influences had included Schiller, Schelling, Fichte, and Hegel and who became one of the most powerful critical voices against "idealistic," "sentimental," and "romantic" presentations of life. "Soul," "heart," and "subjectivity" were increasingly becoming dirty words, whereas "mind, ""objectivity," and "rationalism" were being extolled as ultimate literary and artistic virtues.[32] Such was the cultural and ideological climate in which Goncharov was destined to spend the early years of his creative endeavors. His own position appears to have been more ambivalent and nuanced than that of Belinsky and his followers. What Goncharov would later say about Zakhar, Oblomov's manservant, probably applied equally to himself: "He belonged to two epochs, and both left an imprint on him."[33]

Having started to write poetry and short stories while a university student, Goncharov continued doing so in his spare time. He placed his writings in a handwritten magazine kept by his friends, the Maikovs, who were a well-known family in St. Petersburg, boasting several famous artists, critics, and poets.[34] The only story from that period published during Goncharov's life was his Gogolesque "Ivan Savich Podzhabrin," written in 1842 and brought out in one of St. Petersburg's leading literary magazines, Sovremennik (The contemporary), in 1848. Created in the then fashionable style of "physiological etudes," that is, "naturalistic" descriptions of people and their surroundings, the story is an unexpected linguistic and satirical gem dealing with the amorous escapades of a minor and not particularly bright St. Petersburg bureaucrat. Of particular interest to us in this early work is the masterful naturalness of Goncharov's dialogues, which will show itself so remarkably in his subsequent novels, and the portrayal of Podzhabrin's servant, Avdey, which anticipates that of Oblomov's Zakhar.

In 1843 Goncharov began working on his first novel, Obyknovennaia istoriia (A common story), which was published in Sovremennik in 1847 and made its author instantly famous. Reminiscent in its theme of Flaubert's L'Éducation sentimentale, which was to come later, and Balzac's Illusions perdues, which had preceded it by several years, A Common Story was based simultaneously on Goncharov's own life and, as reflected in the title, on what he believed was the common experience of his entire generation.[35] In anticipation of the impractical Oblomov and practical Stolz, the novel depicted a duo of an idealistic nephew, Alexander Aduev, an aspiring writer who arrives at St. Petersburg fresh from his provincial Oblomov-like childhood, and his older and much more pragmatic uncle, Petr Aduev, a successful St. Petersburg bureaucrat. Needless to say, the cold Russian capital, coupled with the uncle's sobering sarcasm, soon rid the nephew of his unrealistic dreams and provincial sentimentality; yet, as later in *Oblomov*, the tension between "innocence" and "experience" is never fully resolved. The nephew's loss of youthful illusions leads also to a loss of joy, while the gain of pragmatism is accompanied by a dulling of all senses, including love. Many big-name Russian literati admired and praised Goncharov's first novel, but one of the most flattering comments came from an anonymous reviewer, who stated: "The talent of Mr. Goncharov is a talent that is original: he goes his own way, imitating no one, not even Gogol – and that is no small deed nowadays."[36]

Oblomov

> *As soon as I started writing for publication . . . I had one artistic ideal: to depict an honest, kind, and attractive character, an idealist to the highest degree . . . who . . . encounters lies at every step . . . and, finally, falls into indifference, apathy, and helplessness.*
>
> Ivan Goncharov, 1866

THE NOVEL'S HISTORY

An early precursor of what would become Oblomov, the character, appeared in 1838 in the Maikovs' handwritten magazine as one of the protagonists in a story entitled "Likhaia bolest'" (A cruel affliction). This pre-*Oblomov* Oblomov, a.k.a. Nikon Ustinovich Tiazhelenko, was a slothful but rather endearing man, whose last name appropriately evokes in Russian both the attribute "heavy" (*tiazhelyi*) and the expression "slow to move" (*tiazhel na pod"em*).[37] Eleven years later, after the enormous success of *A Common Story*,

Goncharov published a story in *Sovremennik*, "Oblomov's Dream," that would become chapter 9 of part 1 of the novel. "Oblomov's Dream" is Goncharov at his very best, mixing personal and impersonal, comedy and pathos, idyll and unvarnished "realism," nostalgia and social critique, and doing all that without any visible compulsion to resolve what may be irresolvable. Sixty years later another writer, Vladimir Korolenko, would succinctly explain this magnificent dualism in the author of "Oblomov's Dream": "Goncharov, of course, mentally rejected the 'Oblomovism,' but deep inside he loved it with profound love beyond his control."[38]

The work on *Oblomov* continued for several years after the publication of "Oblomov's Dream" but was interrupted, first, by the death of Goncharov's mother in 1851 and then, a year later, by his audacious decision to join the around-the-world voyage of a sea vessel *The Frigate Pallas*, which was sponsored by the Russian government. The invitation to become a secretary to the admiral of *The Frigate Pallas* was first extended to Goncharov's friend Apollon Maikov. When Maikov declined it, Goncharov seized the opportunity and offered himself instead. The ship left from a port near St. Petersburg on October 7, 1852, and for the next two years Goncharov, often sick and exhausted, sailed around Europe, Asia, and Africa, visiting numerous countries, among them England, India, Singapore, China, and Japan. *The Frigate Pallas* ended its voyage in Russia's Far East, near the port of Petropavlovsk, in August 1854.[39] Goncharov then spent another half a year getting acquainted with Siberia and slowly making his way overland back to St. Petersburg, where he arrived in February 1855. During his travels Goncharov kept detailed journals and wrote numerous letters to friends. Much of this material was to appear later in print, first as essays and then as a two-volume collection of travel sketches, *The Frigate Pallas* (1855–57).

Even though Goncharov was not actively working on *Oblomov* during his long journey, the novel appears still to have been very much in his mind, for references to *Oblomov* cropped up frequently in his letters home. Thus he wrote from London in November 1852:

"I haven't given up hope of someday writing a chapter called 'Oblomov's Travel.' There I'll try to describe what it's like for a Russian to reach into his suitcase by himself (and know where things are), to have to look after his own luggage, and to be driven to despair ten times an hour, yearning for Mother Russia, for Philip [Goncharov's manservant], and so forth."[40]

On his return to St. Petersburg, Goncharov first attempted to pick up the work on *Oblomov* where he had left off three years earlier, but then came further delays that he blamed on exhaustion, loss of momentum, a new and more demanding job as a censor, and, more convincingly, the necessity to publish the journals and notes from his journey while they were still fresh in his and his readers' minds. It was during the summer of 1857 when, alone in Marienbad where he had gone to take the waters, Goncharov finally found himself once again in the full swing of creating *Oblomov*. Exhilarated, he wrote to a friend: "I arrived here on June 21 . . . and within three days was so bored I wanted to leave. . . . Then, around July 25 or 26, I inadvertently opened *Oblomov* and caught fire: by the thirty-first this hand had written forty-seven pages! *I have finished the first part, written all of the second, and made quite a dent in the third.* . . . I wrote as though taking dictation. Really, a lot of it simply appeared, unconsciously; someone invisible sat next to me and told me what to write."[41]

By the end of August the novel was complete. Goncharov's enthusiasm, however, was beginning to wane. In September, when still in Germany, he complained to another friend that his novel was "not nearly as good as could have been expected from me judging by my previous work. It is cold, listless, and strongly smacks of an assigned project."[42] He spent the following year revising and rewriting *Oblomov*, frequently professing utter horror at rereading some of its earlier parts: "In the last ten years I have not read anything worse, weaker, or paler than the first half of part 1: it's awful!"[43]

Part 1 appeared in *Otechestvennye zapiski* (National annals) on January 14, 1859. *Oblomov*, as a separate edition, came out soon afterward. The immediate reaction to the novel was mixed. Tolstoy was among its earliest and most ardent admirers: "*Oblomov* is a truly

61821

great work, the likes of which one has not seen for a long, long time. . . . I am in rapture over *Oblomov* and keep rereading it."[44] Dostoevsky, on the other hand, found the novel "abominable" (*roman . . . otvratitel'nyi*) and was resentful that a publisher would pay seven thousand rubles for *Oblomov* while his own works were fetching much less.[45]

WHAT'S IN THE NAMES?

The 1840s, during which Goncharov wrote the initial chapters of *Oblomov*, were in many ways dominated by the presence on the Russian literary scene of Nikolay Gogol and his famous novel *Dead Souls*. Gogol's extremely mobile protagonist is shown to be traveling all over the Russian provinces meeting different characters, all of whom bear "telling" last names (like Sobakevich, i.e., "doglike," or Manilov, the "enticing" one). They also represent, albeit in a grotesquely caricatured fashion, most of the segments of Russian rural society at the time: landowners, small bureaucrats, serfs. The beginning of Goncharov's *Oblomov* appears at first glance to be the direct opposite of Gogol's novel inasmuch as its action takes place in an urban setting, and its protagonist, who is often too lazy to walk from one room of his modest apartment to another, is easily the most immobile character in all Russian literature. But looks are deceiving, for in the beginning of *Oblomov* we do indeed witness a similar parade of characters who represent larger types of Russian society of the 1840s. But, unlike Chichikov, Oblomov does not have to go further than his couch to meet them: they all happen to come to him in rapid succession one late spring morning.[46]

Although it is a typical morning in the life of our hero, since it is past eleven and he is still in bed, it is somewhat more unusual for him to be receiving so many visitors. This is conveniently explained when we soon learn that the book opens on May 1. It is the day of the spring festivities in Yekaterinhof, a picturesque suburb of St. Petersburg, and all urban dwellers are rushing there for fun and entertainment.[47] All but Oblomov, that is. So one by one his visitors come to offer him a seat in their carriage.

The first among them is a young man in a terrible hurry, who thinks life is a never-ending carnival and boasts that his social calendar is bursting with invitations and events. As we have seen in the case of Tiazhelenko, the early incarnation of Oblomov in "A Cruel Affliction," Goncharov, like Gogol, was fond of giving characters "meaningful" names (which do not fare well in translation). Oblomov's first guest is no exception. His last name is "Volkov," or "Wolfman," and indeed, like a hungry wolf, Volkov is voraciously on the lookout for his life's essential sustenance: spectacles, dinners with "important" people, and pretty women. Volkov is followed by a government bureaucrat, a former colleague of Oblomov's, whose name is "Sudbinsky," which in Russian means "a man of fate." Fate has been in fact quite good to Sudbinsky: recently promoted to the head of his department, he can now wait till noon to go to his office and is about to marry a woman whose father will give the newlyweds ten thousand rubles and a free twelve-room government apartment to live in.

No sooner does Sudbinsky rise to leave, than another visitor enters. He is an aspiring journalist and writer who extols the virtues of the "realistic direction in literature" (24), and describes to Oblomov his most recent "social critique" in the form of a story where a small town mayor knocks out the teeth of the local merchants. The author's last name is "Penkin," which contains the Russian word for "foam" (*pena*), and fits an intense and humorless man who seems to be foaming at the mouth (*s penoi u rta*) as he utters his diatribes. It is also possible that Goncharov, who liked to insert English words here and there in his Russian text, actually formed the name from the English "pen," which would then simply signify the man's profession. One of the subjects Penkin is said to be addressing in his articles is "the emancipation of women" (24), and since that topic had strong British roots in the late 1840s, the name could also be pointing to the borrowed nature of Penkin's ideas.

The last two visitors are more of the "regulars." The narrator calls them "proletarians" and laments their parasitic nature (35). They come, he tells us, because Oblomov offers them dinner, wine, and decent cigars in exchange for the dubious pleasure of their company. One of them is so faceless and spineless that he could bear any common Russian name but happens to be called Alexeyev; the other is a menacing boor and a schemer who likes to push people around and whose name, Tarantyev, may, appropriately enough, have links to both a battering ram (*taran*)[48] and a tarantula (which, like Tarantyev, attempts to suck its victims dry).[49]

The names for Oblomov's truer friends are more benign. Stolz is, of course, German for "proud," which is quite befitting a self-made, industrious man who takes pride in his achievements. Some critics suggest that Olga Ilyinskaya derives her last name from the first name of the protagonist himself, Ilya, the implication being that she had been predestined to have her life connected with his.[50] The last name of the woman Oblomov ends up with, Pshenitsyna, is also conspicuous inasmuch as *pshenitsa* in Russian means "wheat," and Agafya Matveyevna is definitely associated in our minds, and – even more so – in Oblomov's, with food.[51]

Then there is obviously Oblomov himself, whose name speaks volumes. It is probably derived from the Russian word *oblomok* (a remnant) which, as in English, often means "a remnant of the past." As many critics point out, though, there may also be other complementary, etymological connections: in nineteenth-century Russian, *oblyi*, for example, meant "heavy" (cf. Tiazhelenko), "fat," and "round," and *oblom*, "an awkward man."[52]

STRUCTURE, PLOT, AND TIME

Vladimir Nabokov once playfully summarized Gogol's story "The Overcoat" as follows: "Mumble, mumble, lyrical wave, mumble, lyrical wave, mumble, lyrical wave, mumble, fantastic climax, mumble, mumble, and back into the chaos from which they all had derived."[53] If we replace "mumble" by "snore" and throw away "fantastic climax," the same summary could be easily applied to the structure of Goncharov's novel. In *Oblomov and His Creator*, Milton Ehre actually comes close to describing the book in a similar, albeit more "formal," manner. *Oblomov*, he suggests, is governed "by the formula stasis-action-stasis" for it proceeds "from dream and reflection to aborted action to a decline back into dream."[54] Goncharov's contemporary critic, D. I. Pisarev, observed that *Oblomov* "has almost no events or action in it, and its plot can be summarized in two or three lines."[55] Another critic writing at the same time chose to juxtapose *Oblomov* and George Eliot's action-packed *Adam Bede*, also published in 1859, as if to underscore that Hetty Sorrel, the heroine of *Adam Bede*, manages to get seduced, impregnated, and incarcerated in perhaps a shorter span of time than it takes Oblomov to go from one dream to the next.[56]

A "sleeper" like *Oblomov* would have been a literary curiosity at any time, but for the first half of the nineteenth century, with its emphasis on *bildungsromane* and novels of education, *Oblomov* must have been a truly stunning book. Goncharov's novel is, in fact, a perfect antithesis to a *buildungsroman* and even a cruel parody of one: despite Stolz's and Olga's best efforts, Oblomov simply refuses to "develop" or "progress" in the manner expected of him as a literary hero. If one can detect glimpses of Samuel Beckett's protagonists in this description, so, apparently, could Beckett himself: he reportedly read *Oblomov* before writing *Waiting for Godot* (1952) and even paid Goncharov a tribute of sorts by giving one of his most absurd characters a Russian name, Vladimir.[57]

Goncharov appears to thwart our expectations not only in character development but also in plot development. Now and then we may think we recognize "traditional," almost Dickensian or Dostoevskian, plot complications, as when the novel's "villains" – Tarantyev and Mukhoyarov – reappear on the scene, intending to defraud and thus ruin the protagonist. But this is just an illusion of a "complication": the fraud attempt does not bear fruit, nor does it affect the protagonist's life to any serious degree. Furthermore, even if we agree with Stolz that certain "ruin" and "degradation" do occur at the end, these are most likely the result not of Oblomov's own action or inaction in the novel but of his nature and upbringing, which seem to have predetermined the protagonist's fate even before we meet him.

It has been a common sentiment in much of Goncharov criticism that *Oblomov* is successful *despite* its absence of a well-developed plot. Typical in this respect is the opinion of Richard Peace, who writes: "For all its apparent looseness of form, [*Oblomov*] is, nevertheless, a coherent and well-constructed work of art."[58] Yet the "looseness of form" in *Oblomov* can also be seen as one of the novel's strengths. Just as he does in his refusal to emulate the then popular *buildungsroman*, here, too, Goncharov may be questioning his readers' assumptions as to the essence of the genre by trying to avoid the predictable plot lines of many other nineteenth-century novels.

Whatever structure and plot exist in the novel, they are indeed quite simple. The novel consists of four parts and spans roughly fifteen years, occasionally flashing back to the hero's childhood and ending several years after Oblomov's death. The main part of the novel is much shorter, though: it occupies spring, summer, and autumn of one year in the life of the protagonist. Spring is the season of slumber and reluctant awakening upon Stolz's return to St. Petersburg. Summer is the season of romance with Olga.[59] Autumn is a return to slumber that leads to eventual death. Milton Ehre was the first critic to notice that these cycles in *Oblomov* anticipate Northrop Frye's 1957 theory of literary myths and archetypes: "The Mythos of Spring: Comedy"; "The Mythos of Summer: Romance"; "The Mythos of Autumn: Tragedy."[60] "Tragedy," however, is perhaps too strong a word for what happens at the end of the novel since some readers may actually agree with Innokenty Annensky, who remarked in 1892: "We have just read six hundred pages about [Oblomov], we do not know any other character in Russian literature who is as fully and vividly depicted, and yet his death affects us less than the death of a tree in Tolstoy ["Three Deaths"] or that of a locomotive in [Zola's] *La bête humaine*."[61]

As Christine Borowec pointed out in her excellent article "Time after Time: The Temporal Ideology of *Oblomov*," the progression of time in the novel is closely correlated to the inactivity of one character (Oblomov) and the hectic activity of the other (Stolz). Borowec also noted that the two characters exist in different "temporal modes" – "linear" in the case Stolz, and "cyclical" in the case of Oblomov:

> Whenever Stolz appears, the narrative jumps forward, as the ratio of narrated time to narrative space increases. Stolz's entrance in the novel marks the end of Part I and its remarkably leisurely pace. . . . By contrast to the symmetrical structure and closure of Oblomov's return to stasis, the progressive advancement and open-endedness of Stolz's movement toward the future cause the novel to open outward and resist the closure of a completed cycle.[62]

NARRATION AND POINT OF VIEW

The narrator of *Oblomov* appears, at first glance, to be a rather traditional third-person, "omniscient" narrator. In the beginning of the novel he is often behind the scenes, largely invisible, and lets his characters do the talking. When he becomes more present, as the novel progresses, the narrator is far from being "neutral" or laconic. He not only describes but also judges, freely calling Oblomov's false friends "parasites" or criticizing Oblomov's family for having been overly protective when Ilya was a child. This seemingly omniscient and judgmental quality of the narrator led many critics to suggest that he does not differ much from narrators found in many other nineteenth-century Russian and European novels.[63] Yet here, too, looks may be deceiving. To begin with, the narrator's strongly developed "moralizing" tendencies are constantly upset by an equally strong note of ambivalence that undermines many of his judgments. The same ambivalence also undercuts the narrator's authorial "omniscience," for it reveals someone who may wish he knew all the answers but is honest enough to admit he does not.

The epilogue plays havoc with yet another assumption the reader may have made about the nature of the narration in *Oblomov*. The man who just told us the story turns out to be a friend of Stolz, and thus an equally fictional character. He is not, therefore, an "undramatized" narrator or "the author's second self,"[64] as the novel until then may have led us to believe. We may assume, then, that

Goncharov is eager by the end of the novel to create an additional buffer of distance between himself and the narrator by making the latter an invented character. It would be, however, yet another unwise assumption on our part. Goncharov, after all, chooses to reveal the identity of the narrator only when the implications of such a revelation cannot affect our reading of the novel – only its rereading. Even more important, in this final act he appears, on the contrary, to bring the narrator *closer* to himself by emphasizing how the fictional author looked like the real one: "plump, with apathetic face, and thoughtful, as if sleepy, eyes" (380). Inasmuch as this description fits Oblomov as well, the same parting gesture is also probably intended to underscore the autobiographical dimensions of the main protagonist.

Other narratorial experimentation abounds. There are, for example, moments in the novel when the "author" reveals himself to us as uncharacteristically chatty, digressive, and not entirely "reliable," in a manner that seems much more appropriate for Gogol's whimsical narrators than for the supposedly more "objective" narrator of *Oblomov*. The best example of that is the beginning of "Oblomov's Dream," where the narrator questions the beauty of seas, mountains, and "wild and grandiose" landscapes in general (in short, the "romantic" landscapes) and extols, instead, the peaceful monotony of central Russia, where Oblomovka is located. While we have no doubt that Oblomov himself feels that way about his native terrain, we are left wondering whether the narrator is pulling his reader's leg.

Some critics believe that to be the case. "The author contemplates the scene with Olympian calm," write Alexandra and Sverre Lyngstad. "The occasional bursts of lyricism are balanced by flashes of irony."[65] Others justify the narrative inconsistencies of this passage by either Goncharov's own antiromantic sentiments (often exaggerated by critics) or the influence of Gogol's narratorial digressions.[66] But we may also legitimately wonder whether we are actually dealing with the same narrator here. If the sentiments expressed in the opening of the dream are so much like Oblomov's own (and, sometimes, even couched in strikingly Oblomovian language),[67] and if it is, after all, *his* dream, as seen through *his* dormant eyes, would it not be logical to assume that the narrator here may be Oblomov himself or, at the very least, that it is Oblomov's point of view that is being reflected? That would not imply, by any means, that the "other" narrator does not share many of the views presented in the opening to the dream – but it would explain why Goncharov might have felt freer to experiment with the Gogolesque narrative technique here than he does in any other part of the novel.

Reflections of other points of view within the narratorial system of *Oblomov* are, while generally overlooked, not uncommon. Thus we often seem to hear Olga's inner voice, as when in chapter 11 of part 2 the evening scene is described through the unmistakable prism of her excitement, anticipation, and anxiety. She and Oblomov have just stepped into the garden adjacent to her summer house. A seemingly "objective" voice tells us that "[a]ll trees and bushes blended into one gloomy mess; one could not see anything two paces ahead, only the sandy paths were winding like snakes in a glistening line" (*tol'ko belovatoi polosoi zmeilis' peschannye dorozhki*) (211). Yet we know that it is Olga, and not the narrator, who is disturbed by what is taking place within her, for she is experiencing a sexual awakening, or "the lunacy of love," as it is called several paragraphs earlier (which will eventually lead to what some have identified as an unexpectedly bold depiction of a female orgasm).[68] It is Olga, therefore, and not the narrator, who, being bewildered and frightened by these new bodily sensations, is likely to see glistening snakes in the dark "Garden of Eden."[69]

All these instances of subtle experimentation with the narrative and points of view should once again prompt us to appreciate how subversive and playful Goncharov could be when it came to the techniques of writing, and how he allowed his well-developed ironic sensibility to question not only the received dogmas of human experience and existence but also the established rules of creating a novel.

CHARACTERIZATION AND DEPICTION

Goncharov was a truly brilliant master of dialogue. It is hard to find another Russian writer in the nineteenth century, including

Gogol, who could exceed him in the liveliness, naturalness, and wit of the characters' exchanges. Like Gogol, Goncharov probably would have made an excellent playwright, but he seems never to have contemplated that route. He was, however, aware that his real artistic strength lay in how well he could hear and represent everyday speech. Goncharov's earlier works – like "Ivan Savich Podzhabrin" and *A Common Story* – often read like plays masquerading as stories or novels. As in a play, characters reveal themselves primarily through their own speech, with the author's comments often limited to "stage directions." While still heavily "dialogic," the language in *Oblomov* is more varied and multileveled.

As discussed above, the colloquial exchanges here coexist with long narratorial passages that characterize the novel's inhabitants more directly. The arrangement of these passages, which in the case of main characters constitute whole chapters, is rather "traditional" and similar to what, for example, Turgenev did in his novels: a character emerges onto the scene and actively participates in it for a while; then the narrator takes us away from the immediate events in the novel in order to introduce the character at greater length, including his or her past. Having done that, he picks up the action – or, in the case of Oblomov, mostly "inaction" – pretty much where he left it.

In addition to the invented narrator of the novel telling us what we should know (or think) about his characters, and the characters "exposing" themselves through their speech, there exists yet another level of characterization in *Oblomov*. It involves the crafty use of "telling" or symbolic objects, of the kind we have already seen in Goncharov's choice of names, where certain attributes to which the names alluded stood for at least one essential trait of the character. Fabulously famous in this respect is of course Oblomov's dressing gown, to which we are introduced within the very first pages of the novel: "He wore . . . a real oriental dressing gown, with no hint whatsoever of Europe" (8). Oblomov temporarily and reluctantly sheds the gown upon Stolz's arrival in favor of a European-looking suit but soon reclaims it as he settles back into his dormant existence under the loving care and supervision of Agafya Matveyevna, who makes sure to wash the gown every time she notices stains on it.

Oblomov's oriental dressing gown should be a private, personal item of his toilet, yet here it carries not only the burden of its lazy owner's plump body but the implications of what is responsible for Oblomov's apathy and passivity. Like Russia which spans Asia and Europe, the Russians, according to Goncharov, consist of two contradictory "halves," eastern and western. Despite Stolz's numerous attempts to activate the "western," industrious, and "socially useful" half in Oblomov, it is the "eastern," indolent, easy going, and dreamy half that rules his existence. If, as a piece of wardrobe, Oblomov's gown is probably not quite as influential as Akaky Akakievich's overcoat, it has, nevertheless, had its impact on Russian literature. Thus Andrey Bely "borrowed" it for his protagonist in *Petersburg*, where Nikolay Appolonovich Ableukhov is said to rise late and spend most of his lazy mornings in a "Bukhara dressing gown."[70] His father, like Stolz, favors social activity and tailored European suits.

The object we come to associate most closely with Olga is a twig of lilac. She tears one off on her walk with Oblomov and gives it to him to smell. Oblomov tells her he prefers lilies of the valley, which remind him of fields and meadows whereas lilacs grow near houses, close to windows, and smell too "sweet." When Olga gets upset at Oblomov's suggestion that, ashamed of his declaration of love for her the day before, he would be leaving soon to join Stolz in Paris, she throws the lilac twig on the ground. Treating the incident as the first declaration of Olga's own love for him, Oblomov picks up the twig and happily carries it home. The following day he brings the twig with him to their rendezvous and announces to Olga that he saved it because he liked it as a symbol of her "frustration." On yet another walk, Olga again tears off a twig of lilac and hands it to Oblomov. When he asks her what it all means, she replies: "As you can see it's a twig . . . of lilac . . . [it signifies] the blossoming of life . . . [and] my frustration." Finally, after Oblomov writes the letter to Olga to persuade her that what she feels for him is not love, she notices the lilacs are fading. Many years later, branches of lilac reappear on Oblomov's grave, planted there, we are told, by "a friendly hand" (163, 171, 184, 204, 376).[71]

Most critics see the lilacs as a poetic symbol of Oblomov's and Olga's love. Some, like Milton Ehre, even gently reproach Goncharov for making the symbolism a bit too persistent, melodramatic, and "strained."[72] What is often overlooked in such readings is that the lilacs are an "acquired" taste for Oblomov, who initially complains that they are too common and too "sweet" but is prepared to love them because Olga does. This, in a nutshell, is indeed the story of Oblomov's and Olga's love, but not quite the same "poetic" version that many critics see. When Olga pronounces that the lilacs signify blossoming and frustration, she comes close to the realization of how unrealistic her expectations of Oblomov are. Just as at first Oblomov is indifferent to lilacs, he is much further removed from both Olga's blossoming and her frustration than she wishes him to be. That lilacs appear on Oblomov's grave is the final irony of Olga's and Oblomov's relationship. "Poetic justice" it may be as a reminder of Oblomov's inability to fulfill Olga's hopes, but that is where the "poetry" largely ends. Far from being melodramatic, Goncharov's portrayal of the doomed relationship is unsparingly clear-eyed, albeit sympathetic.

As Ikuo Onisi aptly points out in his article on "details" in *Oblomov*, the gown and the twig of lilac are, as images, somewhat different in their nature: inasmuch as the gown is a part of Oblomov that stands for his whole being, its relationship to the protagonist is "synecdochical" (and the novel's "telling" names are, obviously, of the same kind), whereas the use of the lilac in *Oblomov* is more "metaphorical."[73] The indisputable virtuoso of synecdochical images is, of course, Gogol who not only created "The Nose" but also managed to describe the Nevsky Prospect crowds at different times of the day solely through their mustaches, sideburns, waistlines, feet, and hats. Goncharov comes close to the brilliance of Gogol's synecdochical characterization when he describes the essence of Agafya Matveyevna through her elbows.

The first time Oblomov sees Agafya Matveyevna it is her bosom, "high and solid, like a pillow of a couch" (324), that he ogles approvingly. By the time he moves in, his eyes become transfixed on other parts of her body as well, especially the ones he sees through a crack in the door as the landlady is working in the pantry or the kitchen:

> Oblomov could see only the landlady's back, the back of her head with a white neck, and her naked elbows. . . . Oblomov watched how she moved her elbows around, how her back bent and straightened again. When she bent, one could see underneath a clean skirt, clean stockings, and round, plump legs.

The elbows present the most fascination for him, however; they become a fetish. After asking Zakhar why she is "rotating her elbows so fast," and getting no definite answer, Oblomov reveals the full extent of his reverence: "Just a small government official's widow but her elbows would do honor to a countess; they even have dimples!" (239). Several pages later he informs the blushing Agafya Matveyevna that her elbows are good enough "to be painted" (247). Soon afterward, he feels free to touch Agafya Matveyevna while thanking her – and it is her elbows he reaches for (263). It is also then that Agafya – probably quite intentionally and subversively – reintroduces the subject of the dressing gown into Oblomov's life, but instead of ridiculing him for it, as Stolz and Olga did, she praises the cloth it is made of and suggests that she can wash and mend it. Oblomov, who is still expected to be marrying Olga at this point, refuses her offer, saying he does not wear it anymore (264).

Soon after Olga's visit to his Vyborg dwellings, Oblomov begins to feel guilty about his interest in the landlady and makes a resolution "not even to glance at her elbows" (276). It is only after he and Olga break off their engagement that Oblomov allows himself to notice the elbows again. But even before that happens his dressing gown reappears. Hours after the end of his and Olga's fateful conversation he comes home exhausted and miserable: "Ilya Ilyich almost did not notice how Zakhar undressed him, took off his boots, and put – a dressing gown! – on him. 'What's that?' he merely asked glancing at the gown. 'The landlady brought it today: she had washed and mended it,' said Zakhar" (290).

In part 4 it is the dressing gown and Agafya's elbows that rule the roost. When, finally, Oblomov confesses his love to the landlady and kisses her on the neck, it is all preceded by him reaching for her elbows again. The scene concludes with a description that sets in stark contrast his feelings for Agafya Matveyevna and those he used to have for Olga: "He looked at her with slight agitation, but his eyes did not radiate with light or fill with tears; his spirit was not soaring calling him to deeds. He only wanted to sit down on the couch and keep his eyes on her elbows" (301).

Ikuo Onisi suggests that Agafya's elbows express the "materiality and bodily presence of Agafya as compared to the spirituality of Olga."[74] John Givens, in the article published in this volume, notes that Agafya's elbows are "at once a provider of food and a sensual object," which, in Oblomov's case, often amount to the same thing.[75] All these observations are no doubt correct. But Agafya's elbows are significant, it seems to me, not only to underscore Oblomov's "elbow fetish" or to describe his vision of the landlady but also to character-ize Agafya Matveyevna herself and even to identify her "strategies" in the battle for Oblomov.

When we meet Agafya Matveyevna, the narrator uses – or even abuses – the word *tupo*, which in English means "dully," "blankly," or outright "stupidly." When Oblomov suggests that he is not willing to move in, she hears him out "dully" and seems to be equally "dully" reflecting on what he said ("Ona tupo vyslushala i tupo zadumalas'") (233). As he goes on with his explanations, she continues to listen to them "dully," occasionally blinking ("Ona tupo slushala, rovno mi-gaia glazami") (235). It thus becomes abundantly clear from early on that the "dullness" of Agafya Matveyevna may stand in direct opposi-tion to Olga's unusual intelligence. Agafya's head, the presumed seat of her brain, is never a focus of either Oblomov's or the narrator's attention. When Oblomov looks at her, his eyes appear to start at the level of her neck, but never above. All we learn about her face, for example, is that it is "simple but pleasant" (233). Agafya is obviously a "doer," not a "talker" or a "thinker." Her hands are her main asset, and if she is to compete with Olga for Oblomov's heart and soul, if not his mind, it is her hands and her elbows that need to be employed. And so they are. In fact Agafya Matveyevna, with her fast rotating elbows, can be seen as literally *elbowing* Olga out of Oblomov's life (*ottalkivaet loktiami*, as Russians would say).

This is not to suggest, of course, that Agafya is a primary reason why Olga's and Oblomov's relationship ends. It ends because it was doomed to fail from the very start, and Agafya is merely a late reminder to Oblomov and the reader that Olga does not, after all, belong to Oblomov's vision of family bliss. As Karl D. Kramer states in his article in this volume, it is indeed Agafya Matveyevna, not Olga, who "embodies those qualities Oblomov had attributed early on to his ideal mate."[76] And yet – as Agafya's subversive actions with the dressing gown suggests – it is wrong to see her merely as a passive figure in determining Oblomov's future. If anyone is passive here, it is Oblomov, while both women compete for him by means each knows how to employ best: Olga through her head and her musical talents, Agafya through her elbows and culinary skills.[77] Agafya wins that battle, as she was probably predestined to all along, since the magical potency of Oblomovka is firmly on her side. But whether Oblomov "wins" or "loses" as a result is, in my opinion, one of the larger unanswered questions in the novel. Oblomov appears quite content in the care of Agafya Matveyevna, who eventually becomes his wife and bears him a son. The reader, however, is made aware that in Agafya's company the protagonist is prone to fall into "dull reflection" (*tupaia zadumchivost'*) (263).

While Goncharov's preoccupation with physical details may be particularly intriguing when they have such symbolic, metaphorical, or synecdochical character, Goncharov's love for the minutiae of life obviously goes far beyond that. He is often as "detailed" as Gogol is, but whereas in Gogol the abundance of often irrelevant details deepens the effect of the absurd, Goncharov's fascination with details makes him, in Yuly Aikhenvald's apt description, "a poet of the room, a bard of the household, . . . a Flemish artist, . . . a troubadour of the everyday life."[78] And although some critics see this quality in Goncharov as proof of his strong "realistic" tendencies, Goncharov's epos of everyday life is in fact much closer in its tonality to that of James Joyce than to any of his own contemporaries.

CONTEMPORANEOUS SOCIAL AND CULTURAL ISSUES AS REFLECTED IN THE NOVEL

Since the articles in this volume focus on many of the subjects presented in the novel, I would like to concentrate here only on those few that are not discussed at great length and that constituted some of the most debated issues of Goncharov's time.

East versus West. The contrast between East and West is a constant theme of Goncharov's works. In *A Common Story*, the "West" was embodied by Petr Aduev, an enthusiastic urbanite and Anglophile, whereas his provincial nephew largely symbolized Russia's tendency toward "orientalism." In *Oblomov*, Goncharov takes this dichotomy a step further by making Stolz not only obviously pro-Western in his views but also half German. Germans, and in particular German tradesmen,[79] had appeared as characters in nineteenth-century fiction before Goncharov as well. Their presence, however, was usually meant to provide comic relief (as in Pushkin's "The Undertaker" or Gogol's "Nevsky Prospect"), supply fodder for parody (cf. Hermann in Pushkin's *Queen of Spades*), or give an impetus to moralistic diatribes (as is often the case in Gogol). Lermontov may have given his readers a rare exception when in *A Hero of Our Times* (1842) he bestowed a German name on a doctor who is almost Pechorin's intellectual equal, yet he also felt compelled to state that, despite his name, Werner was Russian.[80]

Goncharov was obviously not unique in contemplating Russia's future in terms of the Eastern and Western "pulls" on the country. Petr Chaadaev's famous and highly controversial *Philosophical Letters*, largely devoted to this topic, appeared in 1836 in Moscow's *Teleskop*, which was edited at the time by Goncharov's former professor at Moscow University Nikolay Nadezhdin. Chaadaev, who died three years before *Oblomov* was published, postulated there that while Russia, as a Eurasian country, should serve as a perfect bridge between the East and the West, combining the best qualities of both, it had so far failed in its mission. He further identified Russia's main problems as stemming from not learning sufficiently from the "civilized" world of Western Europe while relying too much on its own largely "Asiatic" ways.

Oblomov's Stolz may be seen, in many ways, as a personification of Chaadaev's "Eurasian" ideal. Born of a German father and a Russian mother, he combines German pragmatism and energy with Russian generosity and, to a certain extent, spirituality. The decent, good-hearted, and childlike Oblomov, with his oriental gown and dormant passivity, can also be interpreted as a stand-in for Russia, which Chaadaev and Goncharov both would have liked to reform without sacrificing either her largesse or her innocence. As was the case in *A Common Story*, though, Goncharov does not appear to offer much hope for the possibility of such reform, unless we interpret Stolz as the ultimate prototype for the future Russian heroes who would carry the best that the West and the East can offer. But, as many critics point out, Stolz as a character is too schematic, unconvincing, and probably "un-Russian" to embody this ideal role to Goncharov's – or his readers' – satisfaction.[81]

Serfdom. Soviet critics used to describe *Oblomov* as a novel "which reflected the anti-serfdom longings of Russian society."[82] In 1950 one of them, A. G. Tseitlin, even went so far as to proclaim that "Goncharov never considered Oblomovism a national phenomenon, but strove, instead, to point out its class roots."[83] To be sure, serfdom was a hotly debated issue in Russian society throughout the 1840s and 1850s when *Oblomov* was being written. Criticizing it had become so popular, in fact, that even Nicholas I got into the act, declaring in 1842: "There is no doubt that serfdom, as it exists at present in our land, is an evil, palpable and obvious to all." He did hasten to add, however, that "to touch it now would be a still more disastrous evil."[84]

Unlike Gogol's *Dead Souls*, *Oblomov* rarely addresses the issue directly. The only serf we come to know quite well is Oblomov's Zakhar, who appears not to be too unhappy with his position in life and, like Oblomov, misses Oblomovka with its old, traditional, patriarchal ways of life. The narrator does at times suggest that having been dependent on his masters all his life, Zakhar is like a domestic animal who does not know what freedom really is: "Zakhar loved Oblomovka as a cat loves its attic, a horse – its stable, a dog – its kennel, in which it was born and grew up" (59). Zakhar, according to the narrator, also takes it for granted that his master is a "superior" being (59).

Zakhar is not, however, the "blindly dedicated" servant of the "old school." Belonging "to two epochs" at once, he is full of contradictions. Cranky, lazy, and at times untruthful, he is nevertheless a loyal and even loving servant, with "a boundless devotion to the Oblomov family" (56). Angry when Tarantyev borrows Oblomov's things and does not return them, he is careless with his master's objects in the house, and many of them lie broken. He may make up stories about Oblomov's love escapades, his drinking and gambling habits, to ensure that other servants perceive his master as a "real man," but he actually grumbles when Oblomov does get involved with Olga and spends much time away from home.

Although it is quite plausible that like many progressive intellectuals of his time Goncharov had serious problems with the institution of serfdom, nothing in his novel reads as a strong condemnation of it, Soviet critics notwithstanding. Like Zakhar, who appears to take his station in life for granted, the narrator takes it for granted that serfdom exists. It is Oblomov's noblesse oblige, therefore, that as a serf owner (he has 350 "souls") he should make sure his serfs do not experience unnecessary hardships. In that he largely fails, having entrusted their lives and well-being to a dishonest and untrustworthy bailiff instead of taking care of the estate himself. Driven by remorse – and, even more so, a serious threat that he would be getting less money from his estate – Oblomov spends his (very few) waking hours contemplating plans for improvements and reforms. As much in Oblomov's life, these "dreams" have little to do with reality, and it thus becomes Stolz's task to improve matters some. He does so not by implementing any reforms but by sacking the corrupt bailiff and replacing him with a man he trusts more.

Stolz and Oblomov do discuss possible improvements for the serfs, but Oblomov is, predictably, quite reluctant to change much in the Oblomovka of his forefathers. Thus, on learning from Stolz that a fair is going to be held near Oblomovka, his first thought is that the "muzhiks" are going to become "corrupted": "They'll start drinking tea, coffee, will want velvet pants, accordions, blackened boots – it's all to no good." When Stolz suggests that his friend may want to open a school in the village, Oblomov's reply is equally "un-enlightened": "Isn't it too early for that? . . . Literacy is harmful to a peasant: educate him and he may even refuse to plough."

Stolz's views are decidedly more "progressive." He believes that capitalism should replace the feudal world order and that peasants should be materially interested in producing for the estate owner. He therefore proposes that if Oblomov's bailiff cannot keep the unhappy "muzhiks" from running away, Oblomov should "give passports" to those who are unhappy and let them go. To Oblomov's objection that this way "everyone may want to leave," Stolz replies: "So what? . . . Those who are happy and find it to their benefit to stay will stay; those who do not see any benefit in staying are no good to you anyway: why keep them?" Education, he maintains, is useful for the peasant in order "to plough better" (132).

Stolz's and Oblomov's exchange echoes some of the most pub-licized debates going on at the time. Thus influential Russian folk-lorist and lexicologist Vladimir Dal (who was, like Stolz, half Ger-man) wrote in a letter to a journal in 1856: "Literacy by itself is not going to educate a peasant; if anything, it will only confuse him, not enlighten him. A pen is easier than a plough."[85] Needless to say, this view elicited many responses, among them some quite similar to Stolz's.

Emancipation of Women. The emancipation of women was not debated as hotly or persistently at the time as the emancipation of serfs, but it did figure prominently in the pages of the liberal press. In the novel it is Penkin who first introduces the issue when, in response to Oblomov's question as to what he writes about, the journalist replies: "About trade, emancipation of women, beautiful April days . . . , a newly invented mixture against fires" (24). Penkin's silliness seems to suggest that the issue itself may be a preoccupation of only silly minds. Yet we know from Goncharov's letters to his numerous female correspondents that he himself regarded issues pertaining to the lives of women with utmost seriousness. He may have not been among the most passionate champions of women's rights but he knew that something was definitely amiss in the relationship between the sexes, as becomes obvious from a remarkable letter he wrote to Sofya Nikitenko in 1869:

> To answer such enormous questions as: who is to blame, men or women, for the hideous, chaotic state of relations between the sexes, for their positions in the family and in society at large, for the roles assigned each, and, finally, for the crippled psychologies of both – to answer these questions . . . is practically impossible . . . before the sciences . . . offer us theories about the natures, talents, and abilities of this or that sex, about their differences and similarities, and ultimately about human nature in general. . . . What both sexes *should* do is try to improve themselves a little, be a bit more honest and clear-headed, restrain a bit their animal outbursts. . . . It would be better for men and women to begin improving themselves rather than to argue about who is to blame for what.[86]

Like many of Goncharov's female friends, his fictional women tend to be strong-willed, smart, and full of energy for which they have too few outlets. Oblomov realizes soon enough that Olga may be "smarter than I am" (204), and in that he echoes his manservant Zakhar who earlier came to a similar realization about his wife: "It all of a sudden became clear to Zakhar that Anisya is smarter than he is!" (168). Sometimes these women are born leaders whereas the men to whom they attach themselves lack both initiative and strength. As a result, there often occurs a reversal of traditional male-female roles, as when Olga, for example, thinks of herself as "Pygmalion" and Oblomov, her "Galatea" (186); or when Oblomov declares to her that now "he is not afraid . . . because fate is not scary with you," and she notes that she read these words somewhere, "only there they were spoken by a woman to a man" (204).

Olga craves intellectual knowledge almost as much as she craves love. Lamenting that women are not taught sciences, she often bombards Oblomov with questions that he has no expertise to answer, at which point she becomes angry at him for having squandered the opportunity to learn that she herself was never given. Even her marriage to Stolz, who, unlike Oblomov, can answer most of her questions and is prepared to lead rather than be led, fails to fill a significant void in her life.

Some of Goncharov's contemporaries maintained that the writer based his Olga in large part on Ekaterina Maikova, the wife of his friend Vladimir Maikov.[87] Maikova, who, in the opinions of many, including Goncharov, was an unusually capable and intelligent person (as well as, like Olga, a good singer) apparently could never fill this void either. Several years after the publication of *Oblomov* she left her husband, had a child with another man, and became involved in numerous radical causes, including the women's suffrage movement. In 1869 she joined a commune in the Caucasus.[88]

After *Oblomov*

It is also generally assumed that Ekaterina Maikova served as a prototype for Vera, a female protagonist in the last novel that Goncharov was to write, *Obryv* or *The Precipice* (sometimes also translated as *The Ravine*). Goncharov started working on the novel almost at the same time that he began *Oblomov*, but the novel was not completed and published until 1869. *The Precipice* was special for Goncharov, who later wrote: "This novel was my life. I put in it a part of myself, people close to me, my native region, Volga, my home, in short, all my personal life."[89] Maikova's personal life also found an unmistakable echo in *The Precipice*, where another intelligent and energetic young woman is trying to locate her place in life and society. Like Maikova, Vera becomes involved with a representative of the "new men," or "nihilists," as they were called at the time. Unlike Maikova, Vera, having been "seduced" by the man who espouses "free love," chooses to stay with her family and may be on her way to marrying a person who is liberal yet represents more traditional values. The same year the novel came out, Goncharov wrote to Maikova that his original intentions for Vera were quite different: "My initial idea was that Vera, attracted to her man, should follow him and abandon her nest, and with her maid should travel through all of Siberia. . . . She would have followed him and partaken in his fate, would have been full of perfectly passionate devotion to him, and, if they had no children, would have sought to make herself useful to others all the while, of course, sharing his views."[90]

Critical reaction to *The Precipice*, which artistically is probably the weakest of the three novels Goncharov produced,[91] was quite hostile, especially in Russia's liberal press, which accused Goncharov of turning into a reactionary. This response probably accounts for the fact that Goncharov never attempted to publish another long work, limiting his literary output in the next twenty years to essays, reviews, and reminiscences, as well as numerous articles defending *The Precipice* from hostile attacks.

He retired from his post as a government censor early in 1868 and spent much of the rest of the year abroad. In the late 1870s, following the death of his manservant Karl Treigut, Goncharov, like Tregubov in his own childhood and Oblomov in the novel, assumed the responsibility for the widow and her young children, all of whom moved in with him. He was particularly fond of Sanya (Alexandra) Treigut, the oldest of the three children. An intelligent and tender young girl, Sanya became in many ways a solace for his old age. He repaid her generously by sending her to a good gymnasium and financing her education.

Goncharov died among his adopted family in 1891, at the age of seventy-nine. His friend, A. F. Koni, left a description of his final resting place that probably would have delighted the wry sense of irony in the writer: "When Ivan Aleksandrovich Goncharov passed away, when *a common story* inevitable to all of us, happened to him, his friends . . . chose a place for him at the edge of a stiff cliff, and there now rests the author of *Oblomov* . . . at the edge of *the precipice.*"[92]

NOTES

1. Vladimir Nabokov, *Speak, Memory* (New York: Putnam's, 1966), p. 160.

2. A. P. Chekhov to A. S. Suvorin, May 4, 1889, in A. P. Chekhov, *Sobranie sochinenii* (Moscow: Khudozhestvennaia literatura, 1963), vol. 11, p. 339. (Unless specified otherwise, all translations from Russian in the introduction are mine.) It should be noted that in another letter to the same addressee (Begin. May 1889, p. 336) Chekhov sounded less than enthusiastic about *Oblomov*, which he had just reread. For more on Chekhov and Goncharov, and, in particular, the influence of *Oblomov* on Chekhov's works, see Richard Peace, *Chekhov: A Study of the Four Major Plays* (New Haven: Yale University Press, 1983), pp. 8–14; 82–83. When *Uncle Vanya* first appeared, one critic (I. N. Ignatov) even titled his review of the play in *Russkie vedomosti* (Russian news; 24 November 1899) "The Family of Oblomovs." For Chekhov's largely negative reaction to the title, see his letter to V. I. Nemirovich-Danchenko, December 3, 1899, in *Sobranie*, vol. 12, p. 341.

3. Another rare son of a merchant in Russian literature at the time, Nikolay Polevoy, to whom Goncharov was sympathetic, suffered much derision when he ventured to establish and run a new literary journal, *Moskovskii Telegraf* (Moscow telegraph), in the 1830s. Goncharov often lamented that Polevoy was being called an "ignoramus" despite his vast erudition precisely because he was a merchant's son. See, for example, "Notes on Belinsky's Personality," in I. A. Goncharov, *Literaturno-kriticheskie stat'i i pis'ma* (Liter-

ary and critical articles and letters), ed. A. P. Rybasov (Leningrad: Khudozhestvennaia literatura, 1938), p. 216. Goncharov was also enthusiastic about the playwright Nikolay Ostrovsky, who also came from a family of merchants and featured merchants in his numerous plays (in *Literaturno-kriticheskie stat'i i pis'ma*, pp. 223–24).

4. In "Luchshe pozdno chem nikogda" (Better late than never), written in 1879, Goncharov remembered that "in particular the Slavophiles did not want, so to speak, to know me because of my unflattering portrayal of Oblomov and, even more so, because of the German." In I. A. Goncharov, *Sobranie sochinenii* (Collected works; Moscow: Pravda, 1952), vol. 8, p. 149.

5. For Goncharov's version of this argument, see "Neobyknovennaia istoriia" (An uncommon story), in *Sobranie sochinenii*, vol. 8, p. 249. See also *I. A. Goncharov i I. S. Turgenev: Po neizdannym materialam Pushkinskogo Doma* (I. A. Goncharov and I. S. Turgenev: The unpublished materials of the Pushkin House), ed. B. M. Engelgart (Petersburg: Academia, 1923). For a more recent and very informative discussion of the episode, see Liudmila S. Geiro, "Sud'ba Goncharova: Epizody i razmyshleniia" (Goncharov's fate: Episodes and reflections), in *Ivan A. Goncarov. Leben, Werk und Wirkung. Beiträge der I. Internationalen Goncarov-Konferenz Bamberg, 8.–10. Oktober 1991*, ed. Peter Thiergen (Cologne: Böhlau Verlag, 1994), pp. 25–44.

6. In Avdotya Panaeva, *Vospominaniia* (Memoirs; Moscow: Pravda, 1986), p. 174. Panaeva herself was much more sympathetic to Goncharov than was Turgenev.

7. F. M. Dostoevsky to A. E. Vrangel, November 9, 1856; in F. M. Dostoevsky, *Pis'ma* (Letters), ed. A. S. Dolinin (Moscow: Gosudarstvennoe izdanie, 1928), vol. 1, p. 199.

8. V. G. Belinsky to V. P. Botkin, March 4, 1847, in V. G. Belinsky, *Pis'ma* (Letters), ed. E. A. Liatsky (St. Petersburg: Tipografiia Stasiulevicha, 1914), vol. 3, p. 194. Goncharov, on the other hand, appears to have been far more charitable about Belinsky. In his "Notes on Belinsky's Personality," published in 1881, Goncharov talked about the critic with respect and warmth, remarking that he was willing to tolerate Belinsky's attacks on himself and others because of Belinsky's passionate but also "nervous, impressionable, and irritable nature." Goncharov also wrote that when he argued with Belinsky, he made sure he did it in such a way as not to upset the critic's "emotional equilibrium" or his poor health (in *Literaturno-kriticheskie stat'i i pis'ma*, pp. 196–219).

9. A. P. Chekhov to A. S. Suvorin, May 4, 1889, in A. P. Chekhov, *Sobranie sochinenii*, vol. 11, p. 339.

10. Goncharov, *Fregat "Pallada"* (Frigate *Pallais*), in *Sobranie sochinenii*, vol. 6, p. 106.

11. V. G. Belinsky, "Vzgliad na russkuiu literaturu 1847 goda" (A survey of Russian literature of 1847), in V. G. Belinsky, *Sobranie sochinenii* (Collected works; Moscow: Khudozhestvennaia literatura, 1982), vol. 8, p. 382.

12. Natalie Baratoff, *Oblomov. A Jungian Approach: A Literary Image of the Mother Complex* (New York: Peter Lang, 1990), p. 7. See also John Givens's article "Wombs, Tombs, and Mother Love: A Freudian Reading of Goncharov's *Oblomov*" in the present volume.

13. Quoted in P. S. Beisov, *Goncharov i rodnoi krai* (Goncharov and his region; Kuibyshev: Kuibyshevskoe knizhnoe izdatel'stvo, 1960), p. 22.

14. Ivan Goncharov to A. A. Kirmalova, May 5, 1851, in Goncharov, *Sobranie sochinenii*, vol. 8, p. 278.

15. Ivan Goncharov, "Na rodine" (At home), in *Sobranie sochinenii*, vol. 7, p. 279.

16. For an excellent summary of Freemasonry in Russia, see O. F. Solovyev, "Masonstvo v Rossii" (Freemasonry in Russia), in *Voprosy istorii* 10 (October 1988): 3–25.

17. Several critics commented on what they see as an intentional similarity between the names of Oblomov's housekeeper and Goncharov's mother. See, for example, Milton Ehre, *Oblomov and His Creator: The Life and Art of Ivan Goncharov* (Princeton, N.J.: Princeton University Press, 1973), p. 7.

18. Goncharov, who, like Tregubov, was never married, started his relationship with Alexandra Treigut when he was already in his sixties. Her late husband, Karl Treigut, who died in 1878, had been the writer's manservant. Like Stolz, whose first name was in fact Karl in some of the earlier variants of the manuscript, Karl Treigut was German, and many Slavophiles undoubtedly saw Goncharov's relationship with Treigut's widow as a manifestation not only of Goncharov's bad "social" taste but also of his "regrettable" pro-Germanism.

19. Goncharov, "Na rodine," pp. 279–80. In his reminiscences, first published in 1888, Goncharov changed the name of his godfather from Nikolay Nikolaevich Tregubov to Petr Andreevich Iakubov. The invented name and patronymic may point back to two fatherly, pragmatic characters in

Goncharov's novels – Petr Aduev in *Obyknovennaia istoriia* (A common story) and Andrey Stolz in *Oblomov*. Goncharov liked to be playful with names: in addition to giving Oblomov's housekeeper and common-law wife the name reminiscent of his mother's, he also appears to have split his own name and patronymic between the Aduevs in *Obyknovennaia istoriia*. For more on the latter and possible reasons for it, see Galya Diment, *The Autobiographical Novel of Co-consciousness: Goncharov, Woolf, and Joyce* (Gainesville: University Press of Florida, 1994), pp. 28–29; or, by the same author, "The Two Faces of Ivan Goncharov: Autobiography and Duality in *Obyknovennaja istorija*, in *Slavic and East European Journal* 3 (Fall 1988): 361.

20. Quoted in A. Rybasov, *I. A. Goncharov* (Moscow: Khudozhestvennaia literatura, 1962), p. 7.

21. Goncharov, "Na rodine," p. 330.

22. Ibid.

23. V. G. Korolenko, "I. A. Goncharov i 'molodoe pokolenie'" (I. A. Goncharov and the "new generation"), reprinted in M. Ia. Poliakov and S. A. Trubnikov, eds., *I. A. Goncharov v russkoi kritike* (I. A. Goncharov in Russian criticism; Moscow: Khudozhestvennaia literatura, 1958), p. 331.

24. Mikhail Lermontov, "Sashka," in M. Iu. Lermontov, *Sobranie sochinenii* (Collected works; Paris: Illustrirovannaia Rossiia, 1939), vol. 1, p. 460. Ironically Goncharov, who was Lermontov's classmate at Moscow University, would recall in the 1870s that Lermontov himself had struck him as "sleepy" and "lazy": "He seemed apathetic to me, spoke little, and always sat in a lazy, reclining pose" ("V Universitete" [At the university], in *Sobranie sochinenii*, vol. 7, p. 252).

25. Goncharov, "Na rodine," p. 286.

26. Ivan Goncharov to Nikolay Goncharov, December 29, 1867, in *Sobranie sochinenii*, vol. 8, p. 362. Goncharov's low opinion of the School of Commerce was shared by other former students, among them a prominent Russian historian, Sergey Solovyev, who stated: "They taught us poorly, and the teachers were awful" (quoted in A. G. Tseitlin, *I. A. Goncharov* [Moscow: AN SSSR, 1950], p. 21).

27. Ivan Goncharov to I. I. Lkhovsky, July 2(?), 1853, in *Sobranie sochinenii*, vol. 8, p. 285.

28. The decree is quoted in A. D. Alekseev, *Letopis' zhizni i tvorchestva I. A. Goncharova* (The chronology of I. A. Goncharov's life and works; Moscow: AN SSSR, 1960), p. 17. On Goncharov's graduation from Moscow

University, there was yet another decree, this time from the Governing Senate of the Russian Empire, officially canceling Goncharov's social status as "a merchant" (ibid., p. 19). He was, from then on, identified as a "chinovnik," that is, a government official or bureaucrat.

29. For more on educational reforms at the time, see Nicholas V. Riasanovsky, *A History of Russia* (New York: Oxford University Press, 1963), p. 387–92.

30. For more on Goncharov's experience at Moscow University, see "V Universitete," *Sobranie sochinenii*, vol. 7, pp. 244–70.

31. Whereas in the beginning of the nineteenth century Russia exported 75 million rubles worth of goods and imported 52 million, by the time Goncharov began working in the Department of Foreign Trade both these numbers were closer to 200 million (see Riasanovsky, *A History*, p. 382).

32. For more on that, see Lydia Ginsburg's excellent discussion in "Belinskii and the Emergence of Realism," in *On Psychological Prose*, trans. and ed. Judson Rosengrant (Princeton, N.J.: Princeton University Press, 1991), pp. 58–101; and Irina Paperno's *Chernyshevsky and the Age of Realism: A Study in the Semiotics of Behavior* (Stanford, Calif.: Stanford University Press, 1988).

33. Here and elsewhere, citations are to I. A. Goncharov, *Oblomov: "Literaturnye pamiatniki" Akademii Nauk SSSR* (Oblomov: Literary monuments of the Academy of Sciences of the USSR; Leningrad: Nauka, 1987). All translations are my own. Further citations to the novel will be incorporated into the text.

34. Soon after his move to St. Petersburg, Goncharov was introduced to the elder Maikovs as a possible tutor for their sons. He was hired as such and gradually became one of the family's closest friends. In the 1830s and 1840s the Maikovs appear to have functioned as Goncharov's surrogate family, making his existence in St. Petersburg less lonely. Through them, he also became acquainted with other members of St. Petersburg's artistic intelligentsia, who often congregated in the Maikovs' hospitable house.

35. For an "unfavorable" comparison between *A Common Story* and Balzac's novel, see Mark S. Simpson, "*Les Illusions perdues* and *Obyknovennaja istorija*," in *Revue de littérature comparée* 4 (October–Décembre 1984): 465–70. Although Balzac's influence on Goncharov's first novel should not be ignored, by describing *A Common Story* as derivative, Simpson largely misreads both its very personal and its very Russian contexts.

36. In *Vedomosti S.-Peterburgskoi gorodskoi politsii* (News of the St. Petersburg city police), March 8, 1847, quoted in A. D. Alekseev, *Letopis'*, p. 28.

37. See part 3 of the present volume for a segment of the story (published posthumously and never before translated into English) that describes Tiazhelenko and his Oblomov-like diet and habits.

38. V. G. Korolenko, "I. A. Goncharov i 'molodoe pokolenie,' " p. 331.

39. Most of the crew then transferred to another vessel, *Diana*, and continued their voyage, but Goncharov chose not to join them.

40. To M. A. Iazykov, November 3, 1852, in *Sobranie sochinenii*, vol. 8, p. 280.

41. To I. I. Lkhovsky, August 2, 1857, in *Sobranie sochinenii*, vol. 8, p. 299. See part 3 of the present volume for the excerpt from this letter and other correspondence relating to the creation of *Oblomov*.

42. To Iu. D. Efremova, September 11, 1857, in *Sobranie sochinenii*, vol. 8, p. 303.

43. To I. I. Lkhovsky, November 5, 1858, in *Sobranie sochinenii*, vol. 8, pp. 305–6.

44. L. N. Tolstoy to A. V. Druzhinin, April 16, 1859, quoted in Alekseev, *Letopis' zhizni i tvorchestva I. A. Goncharova*, p. 93.

45. F. M. Dostoevsky to M. M. Dostoevsky, May 9, 1859, in F. M. Dostoevsky, *Pis'ma*, vol. 1, p. 246. Dostoevsky's verdict is not too surprising since, as mentioned earlier, he always maintained a strong personal antipathy toward Goncharov. Yet even Dostoevsky had to admit on occasion that Goncharov was remarkably gifted. Thus, in the same latter where he attributes to Goncharov "the soul of a bureaucrat" and "eyes of a boiled fish," he also states that "God, as if for laughs, endowed him with a brilliant talent" (to A. E. Vrangel, November 9, 1956, in *Pis'ma*, vol. 1, p. 199).

For more on the history of the novel, see a truly exhaustive article by L. S. Geiro, "Istoriia sozdaniia i publikatsii romana 'Oblomov' " (A history of the creation and publication of the novel *Oblomov*), in I. A. Goncharov, *Oblomov: "Literaturnye pamiatniki,"* pp. 551–646.

46. This procession of characters representing different social and official strata is quite reminiscent of yet another of Gogol's work, his play *The Inspector General* (1836), where a small provincial town's "fathers" and citizenry come to visit Khlestakov, mistaking him for an inspector general traveling incognito from Petersburg.

47. One contemporary observer remarked that St. Petersburg was as

empty on that day as "a village during harvest time" (quoted in *Oblomov: "Literaturnye pamiatniki*," p. 650).

48. Nathalie Baratoff also makes this connection between Tarantyev and "taran" in "*Oblomov*: A Jungian Approach," in Thiergen, ed., *Ivan A. Goncharov: Leben, Werk and Wirkung*, p. 199.

49. It should be noted here that with the exception of "Volkov," the "meaningful" names in *Oblomov* are usually quite uncommon. In the case of Tarantyev, for example, Goncharov could have easily availed himself of a similar but much more common last name, Terentyev. By choosing names like "Tarantyev," "Sudbinsky," "Penkin," and even "Oblomov," Goncharov, like Gogol before him, appears to sacrifice the "verisimilitude" of his characters' names for their "meaningfulness." For another discussion of these names in *Oblomov*, see Alexandra Lyngstad and Sverre Lyngstad, *Ivan Goncharov* (New York: Twayne, 1971), pp. 76–78. Their interpretation is, for the most part, similar to mine.

50. See, for example, V. Kantor, "Dolgii navyk k snu: Razmyshleniia o romane I. A. Goncharova *Oblomov*" (Long inclination toward sleep: Reflections on the novel *Oblomov* by I. A. Goncharov), in *Voprosy literatury* (Issues of literature) 1 (January 1989): 177.

51. For more on the "food" implications of Agafya Matveyevna Pshenitsyna's name, see Darra Goldstein, "Domestic Porkbarreling in Nineteenth-Century Russia, or Who Holds the Keys to the Larder," in *Russia.Women.Culture*, ed. Helena Goscilo and Beth Holmgren (Bloomington: Indiana University Press, 1996), where she writes that the housekeeper's name implies "both sustenance and fecundity" (p. 132). See also Ronald D. LeBlanc's article, "Oblomov's Consuming Passion: Food, Eating, and the Search for Communion," in the present volume.

52. For the nineteenth-century usage of these words, see Vladimir Dal, *Tolkovyi slovar' zhivago velikorusskago iazyka* (Dictionary of meanings of the Russian language; St. Petersburg: Tipografiia Vol'fa, 1881), vol. 2, pp. 593, 598. In the entry devoted to "oblamyvat'-oblomok," Dal actually includes Goncharov's coinage "Oblomovshchina" (Oblomovism), which had become a part of the everyday lexicon by then. He defines it as "Russian apathy, laziness, stagnation" (593).

53. Vladimir Nabokov, *Lectures on Russian Literature*, ed. Fredson Bowers (New York: Harcourt Brace Jovanovich, 1981), p. 60.

54. Ehre, *Oblomov and His Creator*, p. 163.

55. D. I. Pisarev, "'Oblomov.' Roman I. A. Goncharova," in Poliakov and Trubnikov, eds., *Goncharov v russkoi kritike*, p. 97.

56. A. V. Druzhinin, "'Oblomov,' Roman I. A. Goncharova," in Poliakov and Trubnikov, eds., *Goncharov v russkoi kritike*, 165.

57. Alexandar Mihailovic discusses the Goncharov-Beckett "connection" at length in "'The Blessed State': Western and Soviet Views of Infantilism in *Oblomov*" in the present volume. See also V. S. Pritchett, "An Irish Oblomov," in *The Working Novelist* (London: Chatto and Windus, 1965), pp. 25–29; and Frederick J. Hoffman, *Samuel Beckett: The Language of Self* (Carbondale: Southern Illinois University Press, 1962), pp. 13–19.

58. Richard Peace, *Oblomov: A Critical Examination of Goncharov's Novel* (Birmingham, England: University of Birmingham, 1991), p. 79.

59. The chronology of Oblomov's summer romance with Olga and some of its details echo Goncharov's own experience when, on returning from his travels, he fell in love with Elizaveta Tolstaya, whom he had known since she was a teenager and who was in her mid-twenties at the time. Their romance also blossomed in the summer (of 1855) during which Goncharov frequented the summer cottage of the Maikov family where Tolstaya was often staying. Goncharov apparently declared his love to Tolstaya after he, like Oblomov, was moved to tears by an aria. It was not "Casta Diva," however, but "Lucia," as sung by a professional opera singer. The relationship continued for several months, but then Tolstaya moved to Moscow and, in 1857, much to Goncharov's distress, married another man. It was partially to recover from that blow that Goncharov went abroad in the summer of the same year. While abroad, he completed the novel, including all the chapters dealing with Oblomov's and Olga's unsuccessful romance. For more on Goncharov's relationship with Tolstaya and its possible implications for *Oblomov*, see E. A. Liatsky, *Roman i zhizn': Razvitie tvorcheskoi lichnosti Goncharova* (Fiction and life: The development of Goncharov as a writer; Prague: Plamia, 1925), pp. 258–83.

60. See Northrop Frye, *The Anatomy of Criticism: Four Essays* (Princeton, N.J.: Princeton University Press, 1957), pp. 163–223. One of the chapters in Ehre's *Oblomov and His Creator* is titled "The Romance of Summer" (pp. 182–95), and he discusses Frye's theory throughout the book.

61. I. F. Annensky, "Goncharov i ego Oblomov" (Goncharov and his

Oblomov), in *Roman I. A. Goncharova "Oblomov" v russkoi kritike (Oblomov,* the novel of I. A. Goncharov, in Russian criticism), ed. M. V. Otradin (Leningrad: Izdatel'stvo Leningradskogo universiteta, 1991), p. 222.

62. Christine Borowec, "Time after Time: The Temporal Ideology of *Oblomov,*" in *Slavic and East European Journal* 4 (Winter 1994): 566, 570.

63. See, for example, Yury Mann, "Goncharov kak povestvovatel'" (Goncharov as a narrator), in Thiergen, ed., *Ivan A. Goncharov: Leben, Werk and Wirkung,* pp. 83–92. Mann dismisses Goncharov's attempt to introduce a fictional narrator at the end of the novel as "very formal, demonstratively formal" (84).

64. For the most part, I am using Wayne C. Booth's terminology here, as found in his *Rhetoric of Fiction* (Chicago: University of Chicago Press, 1961).

65. Lyngstad and Lyngstad, *Ivan Goncharov,* p. 79.

66. For Gogol's influence on that part of "Oblomov's Dream," see, for example, V. Desnitsky, *Izbrannye stat'i po russkoi literature XVIII–XIX vv* (Selected articles on Russian literature of the eighteenth and nineteenth centuries; Moscow: AN SSSR, 1962), p. 302.

67. Compare, for example, Oblomov's tendency to ask himself repeated, often rhetorical, questions and his penchant for exclamations in the beginning of the novel. No other part of the narration is so full of both. Although "Oblomov's Dream" was the first segment of the novel to be published (1849), Goncharov's memoirs suggest that several initial chapters of the novel had been written before the completion of the "Dream" – see, for example, his statement in "Neobyknovennaia istoriia" (The uncommon story): "In 1848, and even earlier, beginning from 1847, I already had a plan for *Oblomov. . . .* Now and then I would sit down and write, for a week or so, two or three chapters, but then would leave it again, and finished part 1 [only] in 1850" (In *Sobranie sochinenii,* vol. 8, p. 251).

68. For more on that, see John Givens's article in the present volume.

69. The existent translations of *Oblomov* fail to reflect the true narrative "voice" in the passage, since they all omit this very revealing reference to "snakes."

70. Andrey Bely, *Petersburg,* trans. Robert A. Maguire and John E. Malmstad (Bloomington: Indiana University Press, 1978), p. 27. Similar to Goncharov, Bely was intrigued by what he perceived as the "compound" East-West nature of all Russians.

71. For a more detailed analysis of this sequence of events, see Peace,

"*Oblomov*": *A Critical Examination of Goncharov's Novel*, pp. 41–46. See also Karl D. Kramer's article, "Mistaken Identities and Compatible Couples in *Oblomov*" in the present volume.

72. Ehre, *Oblomov and His Creator*, p. 184.

73. Ikuo Onisi, "Ob odnoi stilisticheskoi osobennosti v romane 'Oblomov' – Detal' i obraz geroia" (About one stylistic peculiarity in *Oblomov*: The detail and image of the hero), in Thiergen, ed., *Ivan A. Goncharov: Leben, Werk and Wirkung*, pp. 269–76. For another interesting discussion of this characterization technique in *Oblomov*, see N. I. Prutskov, *Masterstvo Goncharova romanista* (The craft of Goncharov as novelist; Moscow: Akademiia Nauk SSSR, 1962), pp. 92–112.

74. Ibid., p. 273.

75. See John Givens's "Wombs, Tombs, and Mother Love: A Freudian Reading of Goncharov's *Oblomov*," in the present volume.

76. See Karl D. Kramer, "Mistaken Identities and Compatible Couples in *Oblomov*", in the present volume.

77. The two women's competition over a "weak" man is somewhat reminiscent of Aglaya's and Nastasya Fillipovna's battle over Prince Myshkin in Dostoevsky's *Idiot*, published ten years later.

78. Yuly Aikhenvald, *Siluety russkikh pisatelei* (The profiles of Russian writers; Berlin: Slovo, 1923), p. 135. Aikhenvald's statement echoes an earlier statement by A. V. Druzhinin, who also compared Goncharov to a Flemish painter. See Druzhinin, in Poliakov and Trubnikov, eds., *Goncharov v russkoi kritike*, p. 171. On details in Goncharov and how they compare to details in Gogol, see also Vsevolod Setchkarev, *Ivan Goncharov: His Life and His Works* (Würzburg: Jal-Verlag, 1974), where he writes: "The 'microscopic' details engulf the very life they are meant to depict; they diminish and in the end devour it. The same device is common in Gogol', who shares with Goncharov a concern with the pettiness of so many people's lives. The crucial difference between them is that Gogol' regards the myriad of petty cares plaguing man as machinations of the devil, whereas Goncharov sees the possibility of attaching a positive value to them" (p. 156).

79. It was under Peter the Great that Germans, together with other foreigners, began arriving in Russia looking for good business opportunities. As Riasanovsky states, "In 1702 and at other times, the tsar invited Europeans of every nationality – except Jews, whom he considered parasitic – to come to his realm, promising to subsidize passage, provide advantageous

employment, and assure religious tolerance and separate law courts" (*History of Russia*, p. 243).

80. It should be noted, however, that the same year *Oblomov* was published, Ivan Turgenev introduced yet another rare sympathetic German character in the person of the composer Christopher Lemm from *A Nest of the Gentry*.

81. Milton Ehre is among many who find Stolz "wooden and unconvincing" as well as a "weak point in the novel." See his entry in *Handbook of Russian Literature*, ed. Victor Terras (New Haven: Yale University Press, 1985), p. 179.

82. This description is found on the title page of I. A. Goncharov, *Oblomov* (Moscow: Sovetskaia Rossiia, 1982).

83. A. G. Tseitlin, *I. A. Goncharov* (Moscow: Akademiia Nauk SSSR, 1950), p. 173. See also, among others, A. Rybasov, *I. A. Goncharov* (Moscow: Khudozhestvennaia literatura, 1960), where he states: "The progressive Russian literature at the time through writers like Shchedrin, Nekrasov, Ostrovsky, Turgenev, Pisemsky mercilessly condemned serfdom. Goncharov joined them. He showed himself as a passionate opponent of serfdom, of 'complete stagnation,' of inertia, of Oblomovism" (p. 126). It is true that in 1879 Goncharov did say that "the reasons for such a state of affairs" as he described it in his novel "all stem from selfsame 'Oblomovitis' (from serfdom, among other things)" ("Luchshe pozdno, chem nikogda," in *Sobranie sochinenii*, vol. 8, p. 159). This is, however, a rather late, post-emancipation admission, and serfdom is given as only one of the reasons.

84. From Nicholas I's 1842 address to the State Council, quoted in Riasanovsky, *History of Russia*, p. 363.

85. In *Russkaia beseda* (Russian conversation) 3 (1856): 3.

86. Goncharov to S. A. Nikitenko, July 24, 1869, in *Sobranie sochinenii*, vol. 8, p. 396. A much fuller version of this letter can be found in the "Primary Sources" section of this volume.

87. See, for example, E. A. Shtakenshneider, who wrote in 1858: "Goncharov . . . read [*Oblomov*] to some of his friends. Someone remarked to him that the female character there was too ideal. Goncharov replied that he had a real-life model for it, and that this original was Katerina Pavlovna [Maikova]. . . . Katerina Pavlovna is extraordinary. She is not at all a beauty, not very tall, skinny and fragile but she is better than any beauty because of her grace and intelligence" (in *I. A. Goncharov v vospominaniiakh sovremen-*

nikov [I. A. Goncharov in the reminiscences of his contemporaries], ed. N. K. Piksanov [Leningrad: Khudozhestvennaia literatura, 1969], p. 59). See also O. M. Chemena, *Sozdanie dvukh romanov. Goncharov i shestidesiatnitsa E. P. Maikova* (The creation of two novels: Goncharov and a "woman of the sixties" E. P. Maikova; Moscow: Nauka, 1966), where the critic attempts to show that Maikova served, indeed, as the prototype for Olga (as well as for Vera from *The Precipice*).

88. For Goncharov's opinion about Maikova's new views and way of life, see his letter to her May 19, 1866, in *Sobranie sochinenii*, vol. 8, pp. 346–50.

89. Quoted in *I. A. Goncharov v portretakh, illustratsiiakh, dokumentakh* (I. A. Goncharov in portraits, illustrations, and documents), ed. A. D. Alekseev (Leningrad: Gosudarstvennoe uchebno-pedagogicheskoe izdatel'stvo, 1960), p. 173.

90. Quoted in Alekseev, *Letopis'*, pp. 181–82. Maikova, who helped Goncharov with the earlier portions of the novel by copying them and giving advice, was incensed by Goncharov's final choice for Vera, and the publication of *The Precipice* marked the end of their long, genuine, and caring friendship.

91. Not everyone agrees with such an assessment. Setchkarev, for example, considers *The Precipice* "[a]rtistically and philosophically . . . doubtlessly Goncharov's most relevant work" (in *Ivan Goncharov: His Life and His Works*, p. 203).

92. A. F. Koni, "Ivan Aleksandrovich Goncharov," in Shtakenshneider, *I. A. Goncharov v vospominaniiakh sovremennikov*, p. 260.

II ❄ CRITICISM

"That Blessed State": Western and Soviet Views of Infantilism in *Oblomov*

ALEXANDAR MIHAILOVIC

Childishness or infantilism has been regarded as a crucial character trait of Ivan Goncharov's supine hero ever since the publication of *Oblomov* in 1859. Readers attentive to Goncharov's promise as a writer were undoubtedly conditioned in this response by the first appearance of the protagonist in the segment "Oblomov's Dream," which predates the finished novel as a whole both in composition and publication in an 1849 issue of *Sovremennik* (The contemporary). In his famous 1859 article "What Is Oblomovism?" Nikolay Dobrolyubov highlights Oblomov's statement to the swindlers Tarantyev and Ivan Matveyevich that he knows nothing about actually maintaining the lifestyle of a landowning *barin* and needs to be advised by them as if he were a child. In a similar vein, Dmitry Pisarev in his review of the novel describes Oblomov as being emotionally stuck in a childlike state, cosseted and spoiled and therefore weakened morally as well as physically.[1] Pisarev takes the same approach as Dobrolyubov in identifying Goncharov's hero as a specimen in a sociological bestiary, an interpretation he reinforces in his 1864 article on Russian drama with the assertion that the Russian so-called superfluous men and the bourgeoisie or *meshchane* are invariably either mental midgets or eternal children, the former laboring under a petty and narrow frame of mind and the latter languishing in intellectual slumber (*umstvennoi spiachkoi*).[2] In Ovsianiko-Kulikovsky's pathbreaking, if opinionated, prerevolutionary history of Russian literature, Oblomov is similarly characterized as having a will that remains in an "embryonic state" (*v zachatochnom sostoianii*).[3]

For all their ideological indulgences, at least in this respect the men of the sixties clearly do legitimately identify an important psychological component of this novel's protagonist. The image of the adult Oblomov as a slumbering child is highly compelling and one that few – aside from critics in our day who assert the complete constructedness of meaning in all textual interpretations – would argue against emanating from the novel itself, particularly from the pivotal chapter in part 1, "Oblomov's Dream." In his 1946 article on Goncharov's novel, appropriately titled "The Great Absentee," V. S. Pritchett (that great dilettante of writing on Russian literature) characterizes Oblomov as one who bears "like a martyr" our secret desire for passivity even as we reject his embrace of it. As Pritchett puts it, "[t]he function of saints is to assuage the wishes of the unconscious, to appeal to that part of a man which is least apparent to himself, and today we must turn away from the heroic, energetic and productive characters" such as Robinson Crusoe, "that too industrious townplanner knocking up a new society." It is "[f]or us [that Oblomov] sleeps, for us [that] his mind goes back to the Arcadia of childhood, drinking the opiate of memory."[4] Writing in the V-bombed ruins of London and in the midst of a Napoleonic reconstruction of England during the nation's political and economic decline, one can easily understand – without necessarily sharing – Pritchett's attraction to the Oblomovian ideal with its nostalgia for a seigneurial golden age perceived to be societal as well as personal. The analogy between the personal and the political – the parallel between the phylogeny of a society's supposed golden age and the ontogeny of the halcyon days of one's childhood – is certainly one shared by both the English critic and Russians such as Dobrolyubov and Pisarev, whose interpretations of the novel continued to be enormously influential well into the Soviet period (and whose own views were, of course, much more skeptically disposed toward that putative innocence of Oblomov's early years). Nevertheless, the particular permutations of what might be called Oblomov's ideology of infantilism underwent a shift in Soviet criticism, reflecting political developments and changing postrevolutionary views on the psychological development of the child. As we shall see, these views dovetail in a curious manner with the philosophical and aesthetic preoccupations of Samuel Beckett, the writer in the West on whom Goncharov's influence was unquestionably the most decisive.

———

In many respects, Dobrolyubov's piece on *Oblomov* represents the most crucial link between Russian criticism of the novel before and after the Revolution. Like many of the men of the sixties, Dobrolyubov is often justifiably criticized for the aggressive tendentiousness and knee-jerk anti-aestheticism of his views. And yet, from a perspective that one would have to call Hegelian, there is some genuine complexity of thought in his essay that has been largely overlooked even by his Soviet commentators. Dobrolyubov underscores the paradox of the puerile helplessness of the patriarchal landowning class, its inability to command any kind of authority. To this end, he characterizes the request of stewardship that Oblomov makes of Tarantyev and Ivan Matveyevich as a bizarre plea for the adoption of him by his social inferiors, paraphrasing Oblomov as saying, "In other words, serve as a master over me and deal with my property as you see fit, apportioning to me however much you find feasible."[5] Although Dobrolyubov could ill afford to be explicit with his radical social views even during the initially heady years of the post-Nikolaevan period, his image of the self-destructing paternalism of the landowning classes and their demotion to a position of moral dependence on their servants and serfs is a potent one in advancing his unarticulated thesis about the necessity of fundamental change in Russian society. This is undoubtedly what he has in mind when he states later in the article that we feel in Oblomov the movement of a new life ("veianie novoi zhizni") that is only hinted at in earlier literary examples of superfluous men such as Onegin, Pechorin, and Rudin.[6] Oblomov represents an unwitting revolutionary, one who brings down the status of the ruling class within himself

and who is simultaneously willing to hand over the reins of stewardship to those serving under him; in this respect, there can be no
question that he represents a historical step forward over other examples of upper-class alienation and superfluousness. In other
words, what seems to be regression is, in the utopian socialist view of
history, in fact a progression. In his 1911 monumental history of
Russian social thought, Ivanov-Razumnik insightfully points out the
subtly individualistic cast of Dobrolyubov's thought, its emphasis on
the category of the personality or individual (*lichnost'*) as the stage on
which decisive ideological battles are fought and won. While Ivanov-
Razumnik is highly critical of all the men of the sixties and is especially harsh toward Dobrolyubov, he is entirely correct in noting this
philosophical difference between him and contemporaries such as
Chernyshevsky and Pisarev who were generally indifferent, if not
hostile, to the vicissitudes of the individual perception in society and
history.[7]

The dialectical subtext of Dobrolyubov's interpretation of the
novel – which results in a curiously sympathetic treatment of Oblomov himself – became particularly important for post-Stalinist
Goncharov scholarship. Strangely enough, however, the dialectical
reading of Goncharov's hero remained a subtext even then, when
presumably there could no longer have been any repercussions
against acknowledging it. Why? For one thing, this idea ran counter
to Lenin's uncompromisingly negative characterization of all aspects
of Oblomovism, which is fully consistent with the first Soviet leader's
highly polemical attitude toward any version of Hegelianism not
specifically rehabilitated and redeemed by Marx. For Lenin, all the
customs and institutions fondly dwelled upon by Oblomov in his
dream are manifestations of serfdom and seigneurial privilege pure
and simple, holding back the transformation of Oblomovka in all its
"stagnancy, immobility and desolation."[8] As Lenin explains in his
lengthy prerevolutionary treatise *The Development of Capitalism in
Russia*, landowners such as Oblomov were able to sustain themselves
only because the corvée system of leveling tithes on their estates gave
them short-term profits without the expenditure of capital. Needless

to say, such arrangements became increasingly unworkable after the abolition of serfdom. According to Lenin and Soviet Goncharov scholars such as Rybasov, who extend Lenin's sociologically allegorical line of reasoning, Oblomov is representative of serfdom in its classic, precapitalistic stage and can only be fully understood in sharp contrast with Stolz, whose mercantilism is ascendant on the eve of the emancipation.[9] From the Leninist perspective, Goncharov's hero is in no sense the historically interstitial and sui generis transitional figure that Dobrolyubov implicitly suggests; nor is the estate of Oblomovka the mythically unreal and historically inaccurate emblem that the early Soviet Marxist critic Pereverzev took it to be.[10] Although this difference of opinion between Lenin and the men of the sixties is subtle, it seems to me to be also highly significant and revealing: Dobrolyubov believes that Oblomov represents as much the harbinger of a new era as he does the senescence of the old one; for him, Goncharov's hero is a personification of a moment in the historical dialectic – the juxtaposition and cohabitation of young and old personae, of the old and the new – as much as he is of a particular class. Lenin, on the other hand, asserts no such duality in Oblomov, who is for him nothing more than a highly representative member of the serf-owning class who, like it, is doomed to extinction. As a reader, even the much maligned Dobrolyubov seems, by comparison with Lenin, to be almost an aesthete in his preoccupation with some of the genuine complexities of Goncharov's text.

Most of the Goncharov scholarship produced during the Stalin era laboriously expatiates on Lenin's uncompromising view. The most prominent example of these treatments is of course A. G. Tseitlin's lengthy monograph on Goncharov, published in 1950 by the Soviet Academy of Sciences.[11] Tseitlin's book is exhaustively researched and contains a great deal of useful bibliographical information about Goncharov. Its high Stalinism and ideological self-righteousness unfortunately make for some painful reading. Lenin is the most quoted author in the book after Goncharov himself, and the whole psychological dimension of Oblomov is reduced to crude allegorizing about class. Interestingly, the whole issue of Oblomov's childishness is hardly touched on in Tseitlin's lengthy chapter about the novel. What we find in Soviet scholarship of the sixties and the seventies, however, is a return to the topos of the childlike Oblomov. In an introductory study to Goncharov's novel published toward the end of the Khrushchev era, one commentator takes a pointedly psychological tack by emphasizing what might be called the etiology of Oblomov's mental debility, describing the impressionable mind of this particular child as tragically absorbing everything negative that surrounded him.[12] Although this statement is of course perfectly commonsensical, we must remind ourselves that its personalism and measure of sympathy were for many years largely absent from Soviet writing about Goncharov's most famous character.

We see an even more substantial acknowledgment of the ambivalence and complexity of Oblomov in Prutskov's 1962 book on Goncharov, *The Craft of Goncharov as Novelist*. Prutskov emphasizes Oblomov's inner slavery (*vnutrenee rabstvo*) in a way that recalls Dobrolyubov's essentially dialectic treatment of the character's psychological duality.[13] The critic also repeatedly stresses Oblomov's inner struggles and the importance of the "specific features of Goncharov's psychological analysis in the portrayal" of his protagonist and even goes so far as to describe the physical details and objects that surround Oblomov as being very much the objective correlatives of his inner emotional state: "material things constitute, as it were, the equivalent image of the internal state of the hero."[14] Although Prutskov does not explicitly refer to T. S. Eliot's quasi-Freudian idea of the objective correlative, he is clearly acquainted with it and gives it a Vygotskian twist by underscoring Oblomov's psychic and intellectual activity (*deiatel'nost'*) in response to the outer and material world and that world's subsequent definition of his thought processes (*myshlenie*). Interestingly, these terms figure prominently in the writings of the so-called activity theory of character formation and child psychology initially formulated by Vygotsky in the late twenties and early thirties and subsequently further developed by Soviet psychologists such as Leontiev and Brushlinsky. As Brushlinsky explains, "[t]he subject not only reveals himself and manifests himself in his

action and in the acts of his independent creative activity, he is
created and defined in them. . . . [H]uman psychology not only
manifests itself, but is also *formulated* in activity."[15] By this line of
reasoning, the lassitude and *in*activity of Oblomov's upbringing (described in his dream) naturally leads to the formation of incomplete
and amorphous thought processes. As Prutskov pointedly puts it,
Oblomov's world is one where there is an absence of the need for
logical thought (*otsutstvie potrebnosti logicheskogo myshleniia*).

In post-Thaw Goncharov scholarship we see an increasing emphasis on the childishness of Oblomov himself, often without recourse to Leninist typology. Writing the introduction to the 1972
collected works of Goncharov, the Gogol scholar Sergey Mashinsky
asserts "Oblomov's Dream" as the compositional, as well as philosophical, center of the entire novel, describing it in terms that are
suggestive of a childhood trauma as well as a collection of attitudes
inherited from social entitlement.[16] In what is perhaps the most
remarkable piece of Soviet writing about Goncharov, Iury Loshchits
in his 1977 biography (written for the series "The Lives of Remarkable People") describes the world of Oblomov's dream in terms that
are surprisingly sympathetic. Loshchits is clearly influenced by the
mythological cultural criticism pioneered by Toporov, Metelinsky,
and Uspensky as something of an offshoot from the Tartu school of
semiotics; this indebtedness and his frequent use of evocative, if
often highly associative, wordplay put Loshchits well outside the
pale of orthodox Soviet scholarship. He portrays Oblomov's childhood state as expressive of folkloric wisdom in its profound organi-
zation according to universal paradigms and archetypes. Thus the
enormous pie or *pirog* that is made in the Oblomov kitchen and that
feeds the entire estate for four days is a symbol of physical well-being
and the abundance of the material world, a cornucopia that is not
only a *pirog* but also a *pir goroi*, an enormous feast. Loshchits asserts
that the entire world of Oblomov's dream in fact represents not
fragmentation, as many critics have stressed in pointing to the possible derivation of the name from *oblomok* (piece, fragment), but also
completeness and the circularity of sated desire. Loshchits states that

the name could just as easily derive from the old Russian word *oblo*, meaning circle, from which come words such as *oblako* (cloud) and *oblast'* (region). He unambiguously portrays Oblomov's childhood as a prelapsarian – one is almost tempted to say prenatal – state of suspended salvific time and not as a kind of anti-Eden or dystopia.[17] Needless to say, it is an interpretation that runs completely against the grain of the older tradition of Soviet Goncharov scholarship.

There is, however, one revealing moment in the novel that has never been thoroughly explicated by Russian criticism. Toward the end of part 2, as he despairs of ever being able to engage in meaningful activity, Oblomov confesses to Stolz that no redeeming fire ever burned in his life:

> It never was like a morning which gradually fills with light and color and then turns, like other people's, into a blazing day when everything seethes and shimmers in the bright noonday sun, and then gradually grows paler and more subdued, fading naturally into the evening twilight. No! My life began by flickering out [*zhizn' moia nachalas' s pogasaniia*]. It may sound strange but it is so. From the very first moment I became conscious of myself, I felt that I was already flickering out [*chto ia uzhe gasnu*] . . . You [i. e., Stolz] appeared and disappeared like a bright and swiftly moving comet, and I forgot it all and went on flickering out [*gasnul*].[18]

It is a haunting image, this conflation of the moments of birth (first light) and death (sunset), this merging of womb with tomb. Viewed from this perspective, the so-called blessed region or corner (*blazhennyi ugolok*) of Oblomovka, in all the mythically hermetic self-sufficiency described by Loshchits, seems less than benign. While commentary on Oblomov's dream from writers such as Pisarev and Lenin do acknowledge its importance for defining Oblomov and the class he represents as stunted children and their situation as a kind of degradation or decline, they do not explore the psychological ramifications of this disturbingly dual image. For that matter, neither does the post-Stalinist writing on Oblomov, which perhaps goes too far in the opposite direction by glossing over and sentimentalizing the dynamics of Oblomov's childhood, a tendency particularly evident in Loshchits's biography of Goncharov and in Nikita Mikhalkov's mediocre film version of the novel. For a meditation on the paradoxes of Oblomov the adult child, we need to look to the work of Samuel Beckett.

The Oblomov subtext in Beckett's life and work has been insightfully noted by a few commentators in the West. In one of the first substantial studies of Goncharov in English, Milton Ehre briefly points out the similarities between the Russian and the Irish writers.[19] Intimating the affinity of Goncharov's narrative strategies with the literature of the absurd, Vsevolod Setchkarev characterizes *Oblomov* as an "anti-adventure novel," one in which "everything that goes into making a novel 'interesting' – dangerous situations, extraordinary experiences, suspense, dynamism of plot – [. . .] has been deliberately avoided," a comment that could as easily be applied to Beckett's *Molloy* trilogy of novels.[20] In an article on Beckett titled "An Irish Oblomov," the ever intrepid V. S. Pritchett paraphrases the perspective of Beckett's heroes in terms that are clearly drawn from Oblomov's famous self-characterization of senescent infantilism: "Why was I born, get me out of this, let me live on less and less, get me to the grave, the womb, the last door, dragging this ludicrous, feeble, windy old bag of pipes with me. Find me a hole. Give me deafness and blindness; chop off the gangrened leg."[21] Pritchett probably perceives the connection between the two writers at least in part on the basis of one of the vagrant Vladimir's statements in *Waiting for Godot* that vividly echo some of the sentiments of Goncharov's often somnolent protagonist:

Was I sleeping, while the others suffered? Am I sleeping now? Tomorrow when I wake, or think I do, what shall I say of today? . . . Astride of the grave and a difficult birth. Down in the hole, lingering, the grave-digger puts on the forceps. We have time to grow old. The air is full of our cries. (*He listens*) But habit is a great deadener. *(He looks again at Estragon)* At me too someone is looking, at me too someone is saying, He is sleeping, he knows nothing. *(Pause)* I can't go on! *(Pause)* What have I said?[22]

It is no accident that these words are spoken by a character with a Russian name, one who describes sleep as a state of innocence or arrested fetal gestation. In another passage that foregrounds a direct reference to Oblomov's famous description of his life as a crepuscular childhood and spent fire, Clov abandons Hamm in Beckett's *Endgame* with the statement: "I am so bowed I only see my feet, if I open my eyes, and between my legs a little trail of black dust. I say to myself that the earth is extinguished, though I never saw it lit."[23] All these associations of arrested childhood in Oblomov's personality have been identified by Russian commentators from Dobrolyubov to Lenin and sundry Soviet critics. What Beckett brings to the fore in his references to the novel is not the class or sociohistorical specificity of Oblomov's infantilism, but rather its universality as an emblem of the human condition, a view that throws into sharper relief his kinship with Witold Gombrowicz, a Polish practitioner of the literary absurd and critic of eastern bloc authoritarianism. Not surprisingly, it is precisely this treatment of existential alienation in Goncharov's work that caught the attention of Western critics and scholars writing during the cold war era.

That Beckett read *Oblomov* before writing *Waiting for Godot* is mentioned by Peggy Guggenheim in her gossipy memoir *Out of This Century* and confirmed by James Knowlson in his recent biography of the critic.[24] The unlikely romance between Beckett the playwright and Guggenheim the wealthy American socialite was not without its own amusing Oblomovesque aspect. She writes that "[my] passion for Beckett was inspired by the fact that I really believed that he was capable of great intensity, and that I could bring it out." In reply Beckett would only deny this, "saying he was dead and had no feelings that were human and that was why he had not been able to fall in love with Joyce's daughter."[25] In January 1938 she received a letter signed "Oblomov" from Beckett congratulating her on the successful opening of her Paris museum. She then explains how this became her name for him:

> When I first met him I was surprised to find a living Oblomov. I made him read the book and of course he immediately saw the resemblance between him and the strange inactive hero who finally did not even have the will power to get out of bed. Conversation with Beckett was difficult. He was never very animated, and it took hours and lots of drink to warm him up before he finally unraveled himself. If he ever said anything which made me think he loved me, as soon as I taxed him with it he took it back by saying that he had been drunk at the time. When I asked him what he was going to do about our life he invariably replied, "Nothing."[26]

As unreliable and self-serving as her memoir sometimes is, this story certainly has the ring of truth as far as Beckett is concerned. In a droll example of life imitating art, Guggenheim places herself in the role of Olga Ilyinskaya vainly attempting to coax Oblomov/Beckett out of his apathy.

Beckett's reply "nothing" is especially significant in the present context. After she fell in love with Beckett, Guggenheim writes that "[h]e was in a strange state" while still assuring her that their life "would be in order one day." As he explained it to her, "[e]ver since his birth he had retained a terrible memory of life in his mother's womb," periodically experiencing "awful crises" when he felt he was suffocating and never "seemed to be able to make up his mind whether or not he was going to have me, but he did not want to give me up."[27] We see this same subconscious antagonism of a insouciantly childlike man toward a surrogate mother figure in Beckett's first play *Eleuthéria*, which was written in 1947 but published for the first time in its French original and English translation only two years ago. A scathing if heavy-handed portrait of an upper-class Parisian family after the Second World War, *Eleuthéria* (the Greek word for freedom) contains in a sketchier and less successful form many of the dramaturgical ideas and even characters that Beckett would elaborate on for the rest of his career. The protagonist Victor Krap (years later developed by Beckett into the eponymous player of *Krapp's Last Tape*) retreats from the demands of his family and fiancée that he live the life of an upstanding bourgeois adult, spending most of his stage time in bed in a sordid rented room. One critic, the Irish novelist John Banville, recently characterized Victor as "a sort of absurdist Hamlet with nothing to revenge."[28]

The references to Goncharov's novel are numerous, beginning with the name of Victor's fiancée Olga (a reminiscence on Olga Ilyinskaya). Victor is characterized as being stuck in a state of amorphous inertia and, like Oblomov, receives multiple visitors who try to rouse him out of his solipsistic daze. As one character puts it to him, "[i]t is time that you defined yourself a little. You are sort of like – what is the way to say it? – like a sort of ooze. . . . Take on a little contour, for the love of God. . . . Why, my friend, you are quite simply nothing, poor fellow," to which Victor replies, "[i]t is perhaps time that somebody was quite simply nothing."[29] Beckett's protagonist asserts the prerogative of not growing or developing, of remaining a child or reverting to one, which is tantamount to being marginal and therefore "nothing" to normal or adult society. In the last act of the play (which begins with Victor muttering in his sleep about his boyhood), he feebly stands up for himself by asserting the freedom of disadopting both one's family and all received notions about identity: "I've always wanted to be free. I don't know why. Nor do I know what it means. . . . First I was a prisoner of others. So I left them. Then I was the prisoner of self. That was worse. So I left myself."[30] For Beckett, the rejection of family represents a step forward into an existentially pure, crypto-infantile state and a step away from stultifying adulthood. As the consummate representation of the perpetual child, Oblomov emerges as the most powerful subtext in his first play.

———

In his 1879 polemical essay "Better Late Than Never," Goncharov describes Boris Raisky of his novel *The Precipice* as a

progression over Oblomov, as a character who will eventually out-
grow the cradle (*kolybel'*) of Oblomov.[31] Goncharov himself acknowledged Oblomov as a transitional figure, as representing the
childhood state of a much anticipated positive hero in Russian literature. The apprehension of Oblomov as an emblem of perpetual
nascence was dimly understood in the nineteenth century. We have
to go to twentieth-century scholars and writers – both Western and
Russian – truly to understand the richly paradoxical nature of this
paradigm in all its troubling ambivalence. In *Waiting for Godot*,
Eleuthéria, and the *Molloy* trilogy, Beckett manipulates the image of
the "superfluous man" that was central to nineteenth-century Russian novels such as *Oblomov*. Beckett himself acknowledged that the
perpetually supine Oblomov was something of a prototype for his
absurdist hero. Nonetheless, Beckett's identification of such fatalistic
apathy as a specifically Russian quality (especially evident in the
character of the vagrant Vladimir in *Waiting for Godot*) indicates that
he, too, saw the Russian character as something fundamentally foreign and strange, as a non-European worldview that takes center
stage during the cultural decline and Spenglerian sunset of the West.
This is especially evident in his short theatrical sketch *Catastrophe*,
which he wrote in 1981 and dedicated to the then imprisoned Vaclav
Havel. In this one-act play a sadistic theatrical director and his assis-
tants – all dressed in the original production like Russian guards and
apparatchiki – brutally manhandle a scarred protagonist wearing a
gown over "night attire."[32] Toward the end of his career Beckett
recast the Oblomov archetype into the mold of a political prisoner,
suggesting a link between the harassment of the individual on the
modest scale of the family or social circle and the draconian demands
of the totalitarian state. Beckett's transformation of the archetype is
shrewd and represents a devastating – if unwitting – rebuttal to the
Soviet bromides about the hypothetical salvation of Goncharov's
hero at the hands of the benignly paternalistic and solicitous state.
For Beckett, the state socialism of the eastern bloc cannot be the
anodyne to the solipsistic fantasy of Oblomov's childhood: even the
"blessed corner" of Oblomovka is superior to the self-anointed

blessed state of political ideology. It is precisely the deliberate attenuation and disappearance of the pure and unencumbered apperceptive sensibility that Goncharov and Beckett decry.

To be sure, many observers of political upheavals in the first quarter of this century saw parallels between the 1916 Irish crisis and subsequent civil war and the chain of events that began in Russia the following year. Both nations were violently transformed into new political orders, changes that invariably recall Lenin's comparison of revolution to a painful childbirth. But metaphors that describe the infancy of nations and states are always problematic in the assumptions they draw about collective identity. Even the militantly pro-Irish James Stephens inadvertently struck a note of sycophantic special pleading and self-loathing soon after the Easter Rebellion, stating that England should grant Ireland freedom "not in the manner of a miser who arranges for the chilly livelihood of a needy female relative; but the way a wealthy father would undertake the settlement of his son."[33] For Beckett, such benevolent paternalism is always suspect. Such paternalism is, however, very much at the center of Lenin's conception of the relationship between the proletariat and the Party leadership. Lenin's likening of real social change to birth pangs is especially significant in shifting the parameters of childhood from the beginning of consciousness to the prenatal state, the new order springing more or less fully formed from the collective convulsions of class uprising and civil war. Lenin sees socialism as the collective manifestation of genuine orderliness and adulthood, and in this regard it is highly significant that he regularly emphasizes the chaos, formlessness, and social strife of Russian life preceding the victory of the proletariat and the true rule of law. In this regard he diverges from the intelligentsia of the 1860s, which (as evidenced by the occasional vaguely sympathetic remark about the character of Oblomov) was fascinated by the highly structured unfolding of progress in history; in contrast, Lenin deliberately avoided any idealization of dialectic stadialism, emphasizing instead its teleological drift toward the end of history in the form of true socialism. For Beckett, on the other hand, contestation in fact continues to underlie structured adult existence. In Lenin's metaphorical and egregiously politicized guise, childhood becomes, in essence, *false* consciousness whereas for Beckett it constitutes a refuge, however temporary, from mutual exploitation. What unites Goncharov and Beckett is the search for alternatives to conventional notions of social agency, a quest that would redefine what it means to be a participant in society. It is this quixotic struggle for the rehabilitation of the subject as an ontological category that takes on mythic proportions in Goncharov and Beckett. Lenin, in contrast, saw this struggle as a passing stage, one that the revolutionary elite needed to work especially hard to overcome. That Party vigilance in matters of individual agency became central to Stalin's rewriting of the Soviet constitution and his redefinition of the rights of the citizens of the state. The excessive privileging of the state at the expense of the individual became the new myth of the "blessed state" of Soviet society, the Soviet counterpart to Oblomov's "blessed corner." This new vision of social consciousness was, in its own way, no less of an illusion than the dream of Goncharov's recumbent hero.

NOTES

1. *I. A. Goncharov v russkoi kritike. Sbornik statei*, ed. M. Ia. Poliakov and S. A. Trubnikov (Moscow: Khudozhestvennaia literatura, 1958), p. 100.

2. Quoted in R. V. Ivanov-Razumnik, *Istoriia russkoi obshchestvennoi mysli: individualizm i meshchantsvo v russkoi literature i zhizni XIX v.* (St. Petersburg: Tipografiia M. M. Stasiulevicha, 1911), vol. 2, p. 59.

3. D. N. Ovsianiko-Kulikovsky, ed. *Istoriia russkoi literatury XIX veka* (Moscow: Mir, 1909), p. 266.

4. V. S. Pritchett, "The Great Absentee," in *The Living Novel* (New York: Reynal and Hitchcock, 1947), p. 228.

5. Poliakov and Trubnikov, eds., *I. A. Goncharov v russkoi kritike*, p. 67.

6. Ibid., p. 80.

7. Ivanov-Razumnik, *Istoriia russkoi obshchestvennoi mysli*, pp. 45–53.

8. V. I. Lenin, "Agrarnaia programma russkoi sotsial-demokratii," in V. I. Lenin, *Polnoe sobranie sochinenii* (Moscow: Gosudarstvennoe izdatel'stvo politicheskoi literatury, 1959), vol. 6, p. 348.

66 : Criticism

9. V. I. Lenin, "Razvitie kapitalizma v Rossii," in *Polnoe sobranie sochinenii*, vol. 3, pp. 311–12, 329; A. Rybasov, *I. A. Goncharov* (Moscow: Khudozhestvennaia literatura., 1962), pp. 128–31, 144–45.

10. For a classically Leninist critique of Pereverzev's attack on Goncharov, see V. Desnitsky, "Trilogiia Goncharova," in his *Izbrannye stat'i po russkoi literature XVIII–XIX vv* (Moscow: AN SSSR, 1962), pp. 299–305.

11. A. G. Tseitlin, *I. A. Goncharov* (Moscow: AN SSSR, 1950).

12. "Vpechatlivyi um rebenka vpityvaet v sebia vse otritsatel'noe, chto okruzhalo ego." A. F. Zakharkin, *Roman I. A. Goncharova "Oblomov"* (Moscow: Uchpedgiz, 1963), p. 78.

13. N. I. Prutskov, *Masterstvo Goncharova-romanista* (Moscow: AN SSSR, 1962), pp. 93–96.

14. "Material'nye veshchi iavliaiutsia kak by obrazom-ekvivalentom vnutrennego sostoianiia geroia." Ibid., p. 99.

15. Quoted in *Post-Soviet Perspectives on Russian Psychology*, ed. Vera A. Koltsova, Yuri N. Oleinik, Albert R. Gilgen, Carol K. Gilgen (Westport, Conn.: Greenwood, 1996), p. 18. For some of Vygotsky's views on developmental psychology that anticipate subsequent developments in the "activity" orientation of Soviet psychology, see especially his monograph *Orudie i znak v razvitii rebenka*, translated into English as "Tool and Symbol in Child Development" and published in L. S. Vygotsky, *Mind in Society: The Development of Higher Psychological Processes*, ed. Michael Cole, Vera John-Steiner, Sylvia Scribner, Ellen Souberman (Cambridge, Mass.: Harvard University Press, 1978), pp. 19–30.

16. Sergey Mashinsky, "Goncharov i ego tvorchestvo," in I. A. Goncharov, *Sobranie sochinenii* (Moscow: Pravda, 1972), vol. 1, pp. 32–33.

17. Iury Loshchits, *Goncharov* (Moscow: Molodaia gvardiia, 1977), p. 172.

18. I. A. Goncharov, *Sobranie sochinenii v shesti tomakh* (Moscow: Khudozhestvennaia literatura, 1959), vol. 4, p. 155; Ivan Goncharov, *Oblomov*, trans. D. Magarshack (Harmondsworth: Penguin, 1984), pp. 183–84.

19. Milton Ehre, *Oblomov and His Creator: The Life and Art of Ivan Goncharov* (Princeton, N.J.: Princeton University Press, 1973), p. 154.

20. Vsevolod Setchkarev, *Ivan Goncharov: His Life and Works* (Wurzberg: Jal-Verlag, 1974), p. 154.

21. V. S. Pritchett, "An Irish Oblomov," in *The Working Novelist* (London: Chatto and Windus, 1965), p. 25.

22. Samuel Beckett, *Waiting for Godot* (New York: Grove, 1956), pp. 58–59.

23. Samuel Beckett, *Endgame and Act without Words* (New York: Grove, 1958), p. 81.

24. James Knowlson, *Damned to Fame: The Life of Samuel Beckett* (New York: Simon and Schuster, 1996), p. 271.

25. Peggy Guggenheim, *Out of This Century: Confessions of an Art Addict* (New York: Universe Books, 1979), p. 175.

26. Ibid., pp. 166–67.

27. Ibid., p. 175.

28. John Banville, "The Painful Comedy of Samuel Beckett," *New York Review of Books*, 14 November 1996, p. 28.

29. Samuel Beckett, *Eleuthéria*, trans. M. Brodsky (New York: Foxrock, 1995), pp. 81–82.

30. Ibid., pp. 162–63.

31. I. A. Goncharov, *Luchshe pozdno, chem nikogda* (St. Petersburg: Russkaia rech', 1879), p. 21.

32. Samuel Beckett, *Three Plays: Ohio Impromptu, Catastrophe, What Where* (New York: Grove, 1984), p. 27. For a description of the original production, see Rosette Lamont, "Crossing the Iron Curtain: Political Parables," in *Beckett Translating / Translating Beckett*, ed. Alan Warren Friedman, Charles Rossman, and Dina Sherzer (University Park: Pennsylvania State University Press, 1987), pp. 80–81.

33. James Stephens, *The Insurrection in Dublin* (New York: Macmillan, 1917), xi–xii.

Mistaken Identities and Compatible Couples in *Oblomov*

KARL D. KRAMER

Many is the comedy whose plot is based on an initial mismatch among lovers. The dénouement satisfactorily aligns the characters into pairs who are mutually agreeable to one another. *A Midsummer-Night's Dream* is a classic instance of such a plot. It might well be argued that Goncharov's *Oblomov* is another example, but without dispensing magical potions until each of the mutually compatible couples are in one another's arms. Thus, ultimately, Oblomov and Olga turn out to be quite incompatible, while Oblomov and Agafya Matveyevna, Olga and Stolz, are wholly compatible. This is a novel of enormous complexity, ranging from the childish to the childlike, depicting a patriarchal society in which the leaders cannot lead but can only be cared for, a society about to undergo a series of momentous transformations. But on the limited issue of compatible couples, the question is this: What determines compatibility? I intend to offer an answer to that question during the course of this paper.

Olga is first attracted to Oblomov by his honesty, his devotion, and his gentleness. She does recognize in him early on those qualities Stolz had pointed out to her, which had made him indeed a lifelong devoted friend to Oblomov. But in her innocence, her naïveté, she has another, less laudatory, aim – to remake him into the sort of man she can admire. There already appear flaws both in her original attraction to him and in her desire to remake him. First, it should be clear that Oblomov will never become her ideal of what a man should be; he comes to her with his own preconceptions of what he wants to attain in life: ease, comfort, peace, contentment. Second, those attractive qualities which she immediately recognized in him are part and parcel of that desire for ease, comfort, peace, contentment that she would alter in him. To replace those qualities with more active ones would surely negate the very qualities she initially admired.

Meanwhile, on his side, are those attributes of a woman that Oblomov has long sought in his dreams. One quality he periodically and rather timidly hopes to find in her is a willingness to give herself up to him: "Whenever Oblomov dreamed, lazily lying down in lethargic poses, in moments of dull sleepiness and in inspired moments, in the foreground there was always a woman, his wife and sometimes – his mistress" (209).[1] To submit to him in the latter capacity is of course something Olga would never do.[2]

But she has other qualities which initially convince him that Olga may well be the woman of his dreams. In the first place, she sings Bellini's aria, *Casta diva*, beautifully. The actual lyrics here are indicative of precisely the kind of peace and contentment Oblomov seeks and which Norma attributes to the moon:

> Chaste goddess, as you cast a silver light
> on these ancient and sacred trees,
> turn your lovely face to us,
> unclouded and unveiled.
>
> Temper, o goddess,
> the bold zeal
> of these ardent spirits;
> spread upon the earth that peace
> which you cause to reign in heaven.

The early stage of their apparent attraction to each other is associated with a lilac branch. The background here pertains to the scent of lilac that first crops up in Oblomov's dream. The scene is a typical morning at Oblomovka. Oblomov is seven, and his nurse, after combing and dressing him, takes him to his mother, who kneels before the icon, puts her arm around him, and makes him repeat the words of a prayer: "The boy repeated them absentmindedly, looking out the window from whence the morning freshness and scent of lilac poured into the room" (111). His vision of the ideal mate owes much to his mother. In fact, one trait of that ideal is the solicitous care with which she looks after Oblomov. Lilac and mother are clearly connected here, and several of his early romantic associations with Olga involve lilac.

Olga holds a lilac branch as Oblomov tries to deny the truth of the word *love* which he had uttered at their previous meeting. She throws down the branch in obvious vexation at his attempt to deny this commitment. That vexation quickly becomes associated with the lilac branch and is itself a sign of her commitment to him, since what vexed her was his attempt to retract the word *love*, which he had spoken the day before. Shortly thereafter he tries to retract his denial: " 'I am not ashamed of using that word. . . . I think it was – ' " (218). But he cannot bring himself to add the word *true*. This is the first instance of Oblomov's peculiar ambivalence in regard to Olga. Nevertheless she understands what he meant to say, and on this occasion they part, having apparently reaffirmed that commitment to each other: "For a long time he followed her with mouth and eyes wide open, and then stared dully at the bushes. . . . He again walked slowly down the same avenue and halfway through it came across the lilies of the valley which Olga had dropped, the lilac branch which she had picked and thrown down in vexation. . . . Happy and radiant 'with the moon on his brow,' as his nurse used to say, he came home" (219). In context, then, the lilac branch is associated both with Olga's hope that he cares for her and with a childhood recollection of his old nurse.

Further references to the lilac branch include his telling her that he had saved it (226); she is knitting a bag with a lilac-branch pattern (242), and she observes that lilac is the flower of life and the sign of her vexation. During this same period in their romance we see Oblomov comparing Olga with his ideal mate, concluding they are identical:

Whenever she appeared before his imagination for a moment, there arose that other image, that ideal of peace incarnate, of happiness, of life: that ideal was Olga exactly! Both images drew nearer and nearer together and merged into one. (213)

But in the very midst of his conviction that Olga is his ideal mate, his doubts persist. At one point he confesses:

"I can't help doubting," he interrupted, "don't ask that of me. Now, when I'm with you, I am certain of everything: your look, your voice, they say it's all true. You look at me as if you were saying, I don't need words, I know how to read your expression. But when you're not here, a tormenting game of doubts, of questions, begins. I must run to you again, look at you again, without that doubts arise." (253)

Within a few pages of making this confession he writes her his letter insisting they bring their romance to an end. He points out, quite rightly as the plot develops, that he is in essence a sluggard and that she is deceiving herself in believing she loves him. What she feels is nothing more than the anticipation of real love. Nevertheless his ambivalence persists, and he hides in the bushes to discover her reaction to the letter. She has, in fact, a variety of reactions. She accuses him of wanting to exercise his power over her: "'Yesterday you needed my saying I love you, today you want my tears'" (265). I shall return shortly to the exercise of power by one person over another. She also accuses him of fearing that he may fall into an "abyss" of activity, which is indeed what she is attempting to lead him into. But finally she uncovers what for her is a positive motive behind the letter:

"In the third place, because in this letter, as in a mirror, I see your tenderness, your care, your concern for me, your fear for my happiness, your pure conscience . . . everything that Andrey Ivanych pointed out to me in you and that I fell in love with, for which I overlook your laziness . . . your apathy. . . . You unwittingly revealed yourself in that letter: you are not selfish, Ilya Ilyich, you wrote not because you thought we should part, that you didn't want at all, but because you were afraid of deceiving me . . . it was your honesty speaking, otherwise the letter would have offended me and I wouldn't have wept – out of pride! You see, I know why I love you, and I'm not afraid of making a mistake: I am not mistaken in you." (271)

But the flaw in this positive explanation of his motives is that his "tenderness," his "care," his "pure conscience," his "honesty" are all part of that same personality which seeks peace, tranquillity, contentment. As noted earlier, it is inherently impossible for her to enjoy the former qualities without embracing the latter ones as well. But at this point she does not see that.

Partially revitalized by her reaction to the letter, he now decides to propose to her. Oblomov's attempt at a proposal has to be one of the most peculiar in all world literature. After convincing her at great length that he has something of enormous import to convey, he stumbles about helplessly, only to assure her that should she fall in love with another he would happily step aside. At long last he produces the words he had originally intended. But this is followed by an apparent attempt to seduce her in the same breath. She responds to his second proposal by saying that those who go down that path end up parting. " '[B]ut that I . . . should part with you. . . . Never!' . . . He let out a cry of joy and sank on the grass at her feet" (296).

But in context that "never" is quite ambiguous. It has acquired a series of other associations before its occurrence here. When they had come to their understanding over the letter in the previous scene, Oblomov had asked for a kiss as a token of "inexpressible happiness." Her response there was: " 'Never! Never! Don't come near me!' " (271). In the proposal scene itself, that previous "never" is responsible in part for his hesitation in asking her to marry him:

"No, no, there is something, speak!" she insisted, holding him tightly by both lapels of his jacket, and she held him so close that he had to turn his face now to the right, now to the left to avoid kissing her. He wouldn't have turned away, but in his ears there thundered that terrible "never." (287)

Thus, by the end of the proposal scene, "never" takes on two opposed meanings: I shall never let you kiss me; "'but that I should part from you. . . . Never!'" This second "never" is separated from the rest of the sentence by an entire paragraph in which Goncharov describes Olga putting her arms around Oblomov and kissing him. And yet that second "never" is also a response to his attempt to seduce her. Thus it is unclear whether Oblomov's cry of joy expresses delight at her commitment to him or some sort of relief on his part that he can avoid intimacy. Why would he want to do that? Because of his persistent uncertainty as to whether she is his ideal woman.

It might be argued that Oblomov and Olga are ultimately incompatible because she realizes he cannot be reformed. In their final scene together she tells him:

"Every day you would fall into a deeper and deeper sleep, isn't that so? And I? You can see what I'm like, can't you? I shan't grow old, I shall never stop living. But with you we would live from day to day, waiting for Christmas, then Shrovetide, go on visits, dance, never think of anything; we would go to bed at night and thank God that the day was over quickly, and in the morning we would awake, wishing that today would be just like yesterday . . . that would be our future, wouldn't it? Is that really life? I would wither away, die . . . for what, Ilya? Would you be happy?" (380)

Olga refuses to play the roles he expects of her. She refuses to be seduced or to join him in his lethargy. She will not submit to his wishes.

Strangely enough, however, Goncharov's novel is built on the premise that the woman must submit to the man. If she does not, the couple is incompatible. To a certain extent, in fact, the roles are reversed for a time in their relationship. As she tries to guide him toward a more active life, it is Olga who, with some momentary success, leads him. But as she acknowledges her power over him, she suggests that this relationship is an inappropriate one: "'Listen, Ilya,' she said. 'I believe in your love and in my power over you . . . but you still have far to go: you must rise above me, I expect it of you!'" (362). Shortly after this Oblomov himself thinks of their relationship, as Olga would have it, with him in the position of authority:

> Both their lives, like two rivers, must flow together: he is her guide, her leader! She sees his power, his ability, how much he can do, and she obediently waits to submit to him. Wonderful Olga! A calm, bold, unaffected, but decisive woman, as natural as life itself! (364)

However unpalatable the reader may find this premise for a relationship between members of the opposite sex, there is a consistent pattern in the novel which suggests that Goncharov accepts the premise.

Certainly, in the relationship between Olga and Stolz, their compatibility is built on the assumption that Stolz will lead in precisely the way Oblomov cannot. When Stolz asks Olga if she will accept his advice, this is her response: "'Tell me . . . I shall follow it blindly,' she added with an almost passionate submissiveness" (434). As Goncharov describes the relationship between them it is clear who is leading, but the path Stoltz leads her down has a peculiarly Oblomov-like tranquillity to it: "She, too, had been walking alone down a humble path, and at the crossroads *he* had met her, extended his hand and led her not into a flash of blinding light, but as it were, to a broad, overflowing river, a vast expanse of fields and friendly, smiling hills" (435). Even when Goncharov suggests she may play as active a role as Stolz, it is still clear who is in charge:

> He could barely keep pace with the agonizing swiftness of her thought and will. The question of what he would do as a family man was already settled, it had solved itself. He had to initiate her as well into his laborious business life because she would suffocate as if there were no air in a life without movement. . . . Nothing was done without her knowledge and participation. Not a single

letter was sent out until she had read it, not a single thought, let alone its realization, was withheld; she knew everything, and everything interested her because it interested him. (466)

When she is overcome by a mysterious restlessness, she fears he may not adore her as he had. But when he gives her a satisfactory explanation of her restlessness, "[S]he sighed, but it seemed more from joy that her apprehensions were over, and she would not fall in her husband's estimation, but would rise" (474). Her happiness is always dependent on his approval. Thus their relationship seems to be determined by his ability always to be the authority figure.

Although Oblomov certainly never attempts to lead Agafya Matveyevna anywhere, nevertheless their compatibility depends not only on her submission to Oblomov's every need and desire but on the happiness that submission brings her: "She had loved him so completely, so much: she loved Oblomov as her lover, as her husband, as her master (*barin*)" (502). In fact Agafya Matveyevna apparently fits perfectly his image of the ideal woman; it is no accident that early on the reader learns that Oblomov's dream always involves a woman, his wife and "sometimes his mistress." Agafya Matveyevna embodies those qualities Oblomov had attributed early on to his ideal mate. She submits to him as mistress, then as wife, and finally completes a triad whose third ingredient becomes clear only in the latter pages of the book – the absolute authority of the male over the female.

If Oblomov failed Olga, she failed him in complementary ways. The *Casta diva* and the lilac were equally fleeting. She was a woman, she might have been his wife, but never would she have been his mistress. He fell under her sway and so could never assume the role of authority she expected of him. From Oblomov's perspective, as well as hers, they were incompatible. Stolz, on the other hand, performs that role which Oblomov is constitutionally incapable of playing: he guides, he leads, he manages to stay one step ahead of her, preserving his authoritarian stance, the stance she expects him to display. And so those who belong together are properly aligned in the concluding pages of the novel, and the initial mismatch has been transformed into a pair of compatible couples in this comedy – at least for Goncharov.

NOTES

1. References to *Oblomov*, here and elsewhere incorporated into the text, are to I. A. Goncharov, *Sobranie sochinenii* (Moscow: Khudozhestvennaia literatura, 1953), vol. 4. All translations are my own.

2. In a recent article, V. Kantor suggests that Olga's surname, Ilyinskaya, signifies that "she is intended for Ilya she is his." My own thesis runs directly counter to this, inasmuch as it is my conviction that the plot shows she is distinctly *in*compatible with Oblomov. When Kantor then goes on to assert that "she is ready to give herself to him even outside of marriage," he is clearly on the wrong track. See V. Kantor, "Dolgii navyk k snu: Razmyshleniia o romane I. A. Goncharova *Oblomov*" (Long inclination toward sleep: Reflections on the novel *Oblomov* by I. A. Goncharov), in *Voprosy literatury* (Issues of literature) 1 (January 1989): 177.

Questions of Heroism in Goncharov's *Oblomov*

BETH HOLMGREN

Scholars of Russian literature like to retell the story of the "Quest for the Positive Hero" in nineteenth-century Russian realism, commending the seekers for their Herculean efforts and declaring the universal truth convincingly embodied in their magnificent failures. The great aspiration of the Russian realists was to envision how man was to live, and the scholars who succeeded Lev Tolstoy's and Fyodor Dostoevsky's crabby radical contemporaries have, for the most part, embraced their novels as the final word. It is only relatively recently that some scholars have ventured to expose the biases of this quest. Feminist critics in particular have pointed out that women writers are missing from the chosen group of "seekers" and that female characters are left languishing on the sidelines or high atop pedestals. They have argued quite convincingly that the quest shunted most women into the roles of symbol or auxiliary.[1]

The issue of class bias has yet to be explored, perhaps because the memory of crass Soviet class reading is so painfully fresh. We should bear in mind that class is neither an exact nor an all-determining category and that Western class divisions cannot strictly apply to the Russian system of estates, but it is quite evident that the problem-tackling, life-questioning heroes assayed by high-culture Russian realist writers tended to mirror and critique their authors' class experience. They were not all landed aristocrats like Tolstoy's Bolkonskys or Ivan Turgenev's Kirsanovs; they could be thinking military men, shabby bureaucrats, or destitute students with the most modest gentry pedigree; or they could stand as representatives of the *raznochintsy*, what historian Elise Wirtschafter has argued to be the most nebulous group in tsarist society, freemen positioned outside the estate system and romanticized as "born democrats" by envious gentry intellectuals.[2] Whatever their significant differences, these heroes shared the common denominators of those estates that did most of the talking and writing for Russian society – extensive education, acute social awareness, and a predilection for solving Russia's ills through social reform or religious example rather than through good business. In the pantheon of Russian realist heroes the peasant may have put in an occasional appearance as embodied "solution," but the merchant, the businessman, the capitalist remained shadow figures at best.

Except in Ivan Goncharov's *Oblomov*. This novel, written in the relatively early days of Russian realism, presents fascinating exceptions to contemporary heroic paradigms, to contemporary expectations that only a noble or intellectual male need apply. Its experimentation begins immediately with the title character, a nobleman who briefly served as a government bureaucrat and who displays certain credentials of the by then renowned superfluous man – intellectual ability and artistic sensibility, dissatisfaction with his professional options, and a critical stance toward his society. The novel processes Oblomov's almost perpetual state of reverie, which climaxes early in his recollection of childhood on the family estate. Yet in lieu of focusing on an intelligent, educated hero clashing with his inadequate context, this text dwells on the protagonist's specific and seemingly insuperable class conditioning. Certainly other Russian realists admitted their gentry characters' self-indulgence and self-delusion (recall the wild debaucheries of Fyodor Karamazov or the bronzed bast shoe in Pavel Kirsanov's study), but this novel itemizes with extraordinary frankness the daily, demeaning costs of being a "thoughtful" nobleman. We enjoy Oblomov's dreams, but we witness from the outset his spoiled body and neglected surroundings; we are never allowed to overlook the "forgotten towel" and "the uncleared supper plate," reminders of the thinking hero's corporeality. Indeed we are subjected to the prolonged routine of his morning toilet at the hands of his serf Zakhar in which the narrator demonstrates at length what he eventually summarizes:

> The old tie between them was indestructible. Ilya Ilych could not get up or go to bed or brush his hair or put on his shoes or have dinner without Zakhar's help. Zakhar could imagine no other master than Ilya Ilych and no other existence than that in which he dressed him, fed him, yelled at him, tricked him, lied to him and yet inwardly worshipped him.[3]

Goncharov scrupulously maintains the juxtaposition of rosy dream and shabby reality, reiterating that Oblomov's meditations are literally enabled by enslaved servants, estate income obtained (and skimmed) by dubious intermediaries, neglect of friends and surroundings, and almost complete inertia. In this Goncharov is more forerunner than anomaly, for certainly both Tolstoy and Dostoevsky explored the same moral dilemma differently. Yet Goncharov markedly deviates in his choice of dream content. Whereas Dostoevsky's dreamers toy with romantic projects of reform or bold analyses of the human condition, Oblomov dwells largely on creature comforts. His dreams anticipate and savor physical pleasures, picturesque sights, delicious meals, and a permanent sense of holiday. The charm of Oblomov's remembered childhood mainly obtains in the "vegetable life" – the routines, rituals, indulgences, and feasts – that enthralls his parents' estate. When Oblomov conjures up a rosy future, he can only distinguish his idyll from his ancestors' pedestrian round of making jam, pickling mushrooms, and boxing maids' ears by its refined consumption and its incorporation of "music, piano, elegant furniture" and a "chef trained at the English Club."[4] Over the rather short long run, Oblomov settles for the baser stuff of his comfort-lined dreams, forfeiting the love of an inspiring but demanding woman, relinquishing his affairs to con men, and marrying his amply endowed cook and housekeeper, Agafya Matveyevna.

To a great extent, Oblomov's descent into the lower class and absolute materiality of Agafya's sphere disenchants the superfluous man, whose charisma obtains in his narrative verve or societal performance. It is almost as if a Turgenev hero had opted to end his days at the dinner table of Gogol's Old World landowners. Agafya, rendered metonymically as elbows and bosom and a facial blank, fits physically into a Gogolian world. But although Oblomov eats himself to death while the righteous chorus of Stolz and Olga looks on in disapproval, it is one of the central paradoxes of this novel that Oblomov *even as consumer* remains so attractive.[5] Despite its vein of self-criticism, the retrospective "Oblomov's Dream," which accounts for "how Oblomov was made," especially engages the reader with its tone of ironic fondness, its fairy-tale aura of harmony and lack of hardship, and its rich detailing of routine:

> No one at Oblomovka ever made the slightest mistake as to where the guests were to sit, what dishes were to be served, who were to drive together on a ceremonial occasion, what observances were to be kept. . . . They would rather renounce the spring than omit baking larks made of pastry at the beginning of March. How should they forget or fail to do it? All their life and learning, all their joys and sorrows, were in these things: they banished all other griefs and worries, they knew no other joys, because their life was full of these vital and inevitable events that provided endless food for their hearts and minds.[6]

Once Oblomov moves in with Agafya Matveyevna for good, it is significant that not only his routine but also the narration of that routine resembles the dream evocation of Oblomovka, what Milton Ehre dubs "a lyrical apprehension of the things of domesticity."[7]

> In March cakes were baked in the shape of larks according to custom, in April the double windows were taken out, and he was told that the Neva had thawed and spring had come. He walked about the garden. Vegetables were planted out in the kitchen-garden; the spring holidays came, Whitsuntide, the first of May, and were celebrated with the traditional birches and wreaths; there was a picnic in the copse. Early in the summer conversation

began about the two great festivals to come: St. John's Day – Ivan Matveich's name-day and St. Ilia's Day – Oblomov's name-day; these were important events to look forward to. When the landlady happened to buy or to see in the market an excellent quarter of veal or to bake a particularly good pie, she said: "Ah, if I only could buy such veal or bake such a pie for the name-days!" They talked of St. Ilia's Friday and the annual walk to the Powder Works, and of the feast at the Smolensky Cemetery in Kolpino. The deep cluck of the broody hen and the chirrup of a new generation of chicks were heard under the windows; pies with chicken and fresh mushrooms, freshly salted cucumbers, and then strawberries and raspberries appeared on the table.[8]

This resemblance suggests a fascinating collapse of class boundaries: Oblomov's people, provincial gentry, have more in common with a collegiate assessor's widow than with the cultivated gentry of the capital. It is up to Oblomov, the next, more educated generation, to leaven this material bunch with enlightenment. Yet despite the efforts of his spiritually mobile contemporaries, he ultimately stays put, ashamed and content.

Most critics judge this immobility as Oblomov's decline; some, including John Givens in his excellent essay in this volume, read Oblomov's retreat into material satisfaction as a classic anticipation of Freudian regression.[9] In either interpretation, we fixate on the infant-reprobate Oblomov at the expense of his less distinct parent-provider.[10] Yet one might also credit Agafya with Oblomov's satisfaction – an interpretation supported by the novel's implicit value system and conveyed subtly by its omniscient narrator.[11] In the novel's purview, beyond Oblomov's objectifying glimpses of elbows and breasts, Agafya expands from body to vision or, at least, agenda. Goncharov lavishes much rapt narrative attention on her housekeeping skills and culinary feats. The passage cited above demonstrates how Agafya's mind-set and discourse (direct and indirect) saturate the narration with details of meal preparation, homemaking, and holiday observance. Yes, Oblomov is duped and fleeced by her class peers, but Agafya's clean handsome body and marvelous housewifery are articulated as positive, if limited, values in the novel. A lesser, but similar tribute is paid Anisya, the inept Zakhar's extremely competent wife and Agafya's devoted partner. Of all the male realists, Goncharov proved most explicitly appreciative of these traditionally female skills, citing Agafya's excellent management and culinary art and recognizing Anisya, through Agafya's eyes, as a "treasure." He thereby tinkered with a heroinic paradigm in which domestic work went unnoticed or agent-less or was proffered as an occasional metaphor for maternity and womanly virtue. As Darra Goldstein concludes in her clever analysis of provisioning in nineteenth-century Russian literature, Goncharov's novel literally "illustrates the ways in which women can use domestic power."[12]

If, among the heroes and heroines of their time, Oblomov surprises with his obvious physical indulgence and Agafya ambiguously tempts with consumable values, the character of Stolz vehemently and systematically breaks all heroic molds. Critics have been quick to dismiss him as a barely fleshed-out thesis, a terribly abstract candidate for positive heroism. The logical, dispassionate exposition of his character and his romance with Olga pales in comparison with the rich detail of Oblomov's portrait, but his biography nonetheless harbors quite revolutionary features. In place of the discredited noble hero, Goncharov actually proposes a successful businessman.

In order to transform a businessman into a hero, Goncharov must somehow guarantee his pedigree. After all, the novel harbors other businessmen who act out its Russian stereotype as unscrupulous schemers, and their presence demands Stolz's immediate and inherent distinction. The story of Stolz's childhood – a purposeful tract – proves he is biologically equipped to balance his father's crude bourgeois German industry with his mother's refined noble Russian indolence; interestingly, his characterization elides German with "burgher" and Russian with "aristocrat." Stolz's ethnic and class hybridity innately ensures both his success and his virtue, heretofore an impossible combination in Russian literature, and valiantly challenges the nobility's seeming stranglehold on heroism. His careful binary recipe also prescribes a blend of refining femininity with regimenting masculinity. Stolz's mother wants to cultivate the inherent "nobility" of his body – his fair skin and small hands and feet – and to instill in him good taste and a sensitivity to art. His father wants to discipline both his body and mind, as befits a working man, and to propel him out into the world. It is his surviving father who largely determines Stolz's hectic life course, sending him to St. Petersburg to make his fortune.

Stolz's regimented construction is essential as a decontaminant. It definitively and repeatedly distances him from his boyhood friend Oblomov, the somewhat effeminate all-Russian nobleman whose soft body lies wrapped in a shapeless dressing gown. (Stolz rides off to Petersburg with two wardrobes – rough workclothes and fancy dress.)[13] The reader has lolled about with Oblomov for 150 pages before Stolz enters in a classically heroic mode, vigorous, questing, and ready to cross boundaries and shake things up. Stolz's heroism truly depends on Oblomov's demotion. In the nineteenth-century Russian context, a businessman dealing always with the buying and selling of goods can impress only if the other protagonists are more matter-bound than he. Quite deliberately Goncharov never lets us know what Stolz's business is, nor do we see him in action; such prosaic and demeaning details are omitted. What we mainly know is that business sets Stolz in motion, in contrast to Oblomov, and that Stolz is less a consumer than a circulator. He accrues a fortune for want of having something to do, not for want of something to have, and he readily shares his wealth with those who need it. In this connection it is also important that Stolz actively opposes the unscrupulous Tarantyev, discovering, punishing, and compensating for his embezzlement of Oblomov's funds. Throughout the novel Stolz is depicted as a caretaker and a donor. Characteristically his final acts include adopting Oblomov's and Agafya's son, offering money and a home to the abandoned Zakhar, and entrusting Oblomov's life story to the narrator.

This noted, I do agree with the many critics who declare Stolz too good to be true. He projects the packaging of didactic or even socialist realist fiction. And his obviously rigged success story simply cannot compete with Oblomov's appealing and genuine failure. But his cardboard characterization does not necessarily mean that he would be dismissed by the general reading public. The heroes in Nikolay Chernyshevsky's *What Is to Be Done?* are likewise unconvincing and programmatically drawn, but in their case the novelist's artistic flaws did not impede their extraordinary influence. We perhaps cannot know how Stolz was generally received, but it is telling that Nikolay Dobrolyubov's famous analysis of the novel – "What is Oblomovitis?" – not only points out the implausibility of Stolz's success but also casts aspersions on his real-life class. Dobrolyubov pronounces Stolz premature for "the educated section of society, which is capable of loftier strivings; among the masses, where ideas and strivings are confined to a few and very practical objects, we constantly come across such people" (171).[14] In an illuminating self-contradiction, the radical critic admits that Stolz could be drawn from life but not from the nobility, and that, he implies, means that Stolz cannot function as a hero. Stolz fails as both artistic creation and role model; his constructed classiness does not convince the *raznochinets* critic.

In yet another surprising aperçu Dobrolyubov suggests that the novel's true hero may be none other than Olga Ilyinskaya, Oblomov's disappointed fiancée and Stolz's eventual wife. He celebrates her as both good and real:

> In intellectual development, Olga is the highest ideal that a Russian artist can find in our present Russian life. That is why the extraordinary clarity and simplicity of her logic and the amazing harmony of heart and mind astonish us so much that we are ready to doubt even her imaginary existence and say, "There are no such young women." But following her through the whole novel, we find that she is always true to herself and to her development, that she is not merely the creation of the author, but a living person, though one we have not yet met.[15]

It is not altogether clear why Dobrolyubov saw Olga as real, although male critics of the period often allowed female characters a greater margin of implausible virtue because they read them myopically or as convenient symbols. He defends himself by remarking that female readers ("ladies") share his opinion. Other critics, however, have paired Olga with the "inauthentic" Stolz. D. S. Mirsky, for example, deems Olga "unconvincing" and the Olga-Oblomov romance "inadequate."[16] Goncharov does draw Olga's character schematically, although without Stolz's obvious and unerring syntheses. She is present more as potential than solution. Milton Ehre argues that her orphanhood and lack of a family past provide "a fundamental premise upon which the didacticism of the novel depends" (204).

But Olga nonetheless actualizes an unusual position for a heroine in a male-authored Russian realist novel. Dobrolyubov discerns this as he favorably compares her to her victimized fictional predecessors – Alexander Pushkin's Tatyana in *Eugene Onegin*, Mikhail Lermontov's Princess Mary in *A Hero of Our Time*, and Turgenev's Natalya in *Rudin*. For all Oblomov's charm and Stolz's mobility, Olga emerges as the one protagonist who intuits and follows her own course of spiritual action. She reverses and revises male-female roles in playing Pygmalion to Oblomov's unprepossessing Galatea. She is no provincial maiden aroused by a charismatic visitor; rather, it is *she* who arouses, educates, and *leaves* because of what she believes in and desires. Although her course as a nineteenth-century heroine must be more socially and professionally circumscribed than that of a nineteenth-century hero, her perpetual restlessness tacitly critiques this status quo and distinguishes her from both Oblomov and Stolz. Olga knows that in marrying a man she marries a way of life, and we are unexpectedly privy to her calculations to improve both her man and her future. Such revelations distinguish Olga from other male-authored realist heroines because she is neither blinded by love nor mentored by her lover.

More astonishing, however, is the fact that happy marriage and motherhood do not settle this heroine down. We are primed to accept her parting with the lethargic Oblomov, but her dissatisfaction with the model Stolz is unprecedented. I cannot think of another instance in male-authored Russian realism in which a wife is shown so consistently to be the couple's troubled seeker. In these texts marriage generally seals the heroine's spiritual development.[17] When Olga laments that her monotonous domestic routine is "the end of the road," she recalls Tolstoy's Konstantin Levin, not Kitty Shcherbatsky, and certainly not Natasha Rostova. Nor is she distorted into oddity or perverse femme fatale, like the sexually knowledgeable women who perplex and frighten in Dostoevsky's and Turgenev's works.[18] Although Goncharov ultimately silences her with Stolz's pat counsel and overshadows her with Oblomov's "decline," he has allowed her to move actively beyond extant roles of captivated maiden, long-suffering good woman, and preserver of the family hearth.[19] Once again Goncharov toys with the possibility of a different sort of heroine, only this time the heroine momentarily "womans" the Russian realist hero's quest.

Charming glutton, ennobled businessman, powerful cook, spiritually questing wife and mother – what accounts for Goncharov's innovative and somewhat inadvertent heroes and heroines? What led him to experiment with the conventional notions of class and gendered experience and accomplishment, at least as these were inscribed in Russian fiction? We might subscribe to D. S. Mirsky's cranky judgment – that Goncharov sometimes wrote like the "small" bureaucrat he was, forced to substitute paper solutions for real art.[20] Or we might entertain the curious theory of a 1937 doctoral candidate at Columbia University, whose book valorizing the businessman in Russian literature ascribes both the heroic Stolz and the failed Oblomov to Goncharov's merchant background.[21] But rather than succumb to that always tantalizing sin of essentialism, I think the evidence of his realist text shows that Goncharov, for whatever combination of biographical influences, was clearly alive to differences of class and gender in Russian society that were either overlooked or dismissed by those writers who have heretofore endured as authoritative in the Russian realist canon. And I suggest that we read and teach Oblomov less for its famous failure to construct a persuasive positive hero, and more for the intriguing heroic and heroinic alternatives it sometimes explores and more often indulgently admits. Goncharov did not feel comfortable pronouncing them all heroes. Only Stolz retains that honor. But the author could not deny his other vivid characters' appeal and a great many loose ends. It is no accident that as Stolz unequivocably steps into the roles of exemplar and judge, his meddling most irritates and most predisposes us to like his flawed beneficiaries – the unambitious and life-loving Oblomov, the humble kitchen wizard Agafya, and the troubled, impetuous, vital Olga. With all its stated intentions and disclosed affections, Goncharov's novel leads us to question realist presumptions about the noble Russian hero, to consider not only new candidates for the job but different job descriptions altogether.

NOTES

1. The first such exposé appeared in Barbara Heldt's pioneering study, *Terrible Perfection: Women and Russian Literature* (Bloomington: Indiana University Press, 1987). In her trenchant essay, "The Superfluous Man and the Necessary Woman: A 'Re-vision,'" *The Russian Review* 55 (April 1996): 226–44, Jehanne Gheith traces the accessory plot of the heroine "created as a counterpart to the superfluous man, both as his ideal (she embodies the values to which he aspires) and as the measure of his superfluity (it is when she asks him to make a decision, usually to marry her, that he must face the fact that he is incapable of action)" (232). See also Jane Costlow's perceptive mapping of the rather different heroinic models proposed by women writers of Russian realism: "Love, Work, and the Woman Question in Mid-Nineteenth Century Women's Writing," in *Women Writers in Russian Literature*, ed. Toby Clyman and Diana Greene (Westport, Conn.: Greenwood, 1994), 61–75.

2. Elise Wirtschafter, *Structures of Society: Imperial Russia's "People of Various Ranks"* (DeKalb: Northern Illinois University Press, 1994).

3. All quotations taken from *Oblomov*, trans. Natalie Duddington (New York: Dutton, 1953), with my occasional revisions based on the Russian text

included in I. A. Goncharov's *Sobranie sochinenii*, vol. 4 (Moscow: Khudo-zhestvennaia literatura, 1979). Eng., 71; Russ., 76.

4. Eng., 182; Russ., 182.

5. In his foundational study of Goncharov's works, Milton Ehre traces this attraction more generally to the "paradox of childhood" in *Oblomov and His Creator: The Life and Art of Ivan Goncharov* (Princeton, N.J.: Princeton University Press, 1973), p. 219. I would add that Goncharov's rendering of childhood values emphasizes creature comforts and consumption rather than the full gamut of childhood experience.

6. Eng., 119; Russ., 125–26.

7. Ehre, *Oblomov and His Creator*, 215.

8. Eng., 392–93; Russ., 381. For a fascinating discussion of the symbolism of food in Oblomov's life, see Ronald D. LeBlanc's article in this volume, "Oblomov's Consuming Passion: Food, Eating, and the Search for Communion."

9. Cf. John Givens, "Wombs, Tombs, and Mother Love: A Freudian Reading of Goncharov's *Oblomov*," in the present volume.

10. In this sense, while Freudian readings of *Oblomov* highlight Goncharov's psychological perspicacity, they tend to reinforce critical neglect of his quite extraordinary female characterizations, much as Freud overlooked women by mapping the psyche from a supposedly "universal" male point of view.

11. Ehre, in *Oblomov and His Creator*, makes a more general observation: "The very objects intended to denote Oblomov's fall from grace are often treated in a manner subversive of the intention" (214).

12. Darra Goldstein, "Domestic Porkbarreling in Nineteenth-Century Russia, or Who Holds the Keys to the Larder?" in *Russia.Women.Culture*, ed. Helena Goscilo and Beth Holmgren (Bloomington: Indiana University Press, 1996), p. 132.

13. As I have already noted, Goncharov's distinctive embodying of his characters has prompted psychoanalytical readings of the novel. Although the scope of this article does not permit me this tangent, it would be intriguing to trace the novelist's experimentation with notions of the hero's desired and/or attractive sexuality.

14. Cited in N. A. Dobrolyubov's "What Is Oblomovitis?" in *Belinsky, Chernyshevsky, and Dobrolyubov: Selected Criticism*, ed. and with an intro. by

Ralph E. Matlaw (Bloomington: Indiana University Press, 1976), pp. 133–75.

15. Dobrolyubov, "What Is Oblomovitis?" 172.

16. D. S. Mirsky, *A History of Russian Literature from Its Beginnings to 1900*, ed. Francis J. Whitfield (New York: Vintage, 1958), p. 192.

17. Gheith notes that most heroines in superfluous-man narratives hover "on the border between girlhood and womanhood" ("The Superfluous Man and the Necessary Woman," 234).

18. See Costlow's analysis of the peculiar case of another female anomaly – Anna Odintsova in Turgenev's *Fathers and Children*. "'Oh-La-La' and 'No-No-No': Odintsova as Woman Alone in *Fathers and Children*," in *A Plot of Her Own: The Female Protagonist in Russian Literature*, ed. Sona Stephan Hoisington (Evanston, Ill.: Northwestern University Press, 1995), 21–32. One other possible exception to this pattern can be found in an earlier Goncharov heroine, the wife of Petr Aduev in *A Common Story*; this wife's dissatisfaction results in the husband's retirement and their relocation abroad. I am grateful to Galya Diment for this observation.

19. In this sense my reading departs somewhat from the argument expressed in Karl D. Kramer's essay in this volume. I agree with Kramer that Olga's ultimate fate and intermittent insistence on Oblomov's assuming superiority over her underscore the premise, held by most of Russian educated society, that the woman must submit to the man. But, as in the Stolz/Oblomov pairing, I think Goncharov's thesis backfires in complex and compelling characterization: Olga's vivacious, questing character is so drawn as to chafe against both Oblomov's and Stolz's inadequacies. Goncharov does not seem able to imagine her well as the submissive party. For another discussion of Goncharov's view of Olga, see Galya Diment, "The Precocious Talent of Ivan Goncharov," in the present volume.

20. Mirsky, *A History of Russian Literature*, 192.

21. Cf. Louis Perlman, *Russian Literature and the Business Man* (New York: Columbia University Press, 1937).

Wombs, Tombs, and Mother Love: A Freudian Reading of Goncharov's *Oblomov*

JOHN GIVENS

On the edges of love's idyll, as well as on the edges of the idyll of childhood, stand prohibitive and inhibiting sentinels.
Milton Ehre

Ivan Goncharov's *Oblomov* is a disturbing book. Indeed it is surprising that so few studies have dwelt on this fact. Distracted by the humorous figure of a hero who cannot get out of bed or preconditioned to read the novel as a social document, we pay less attention to aspects of the novel that are troubling on a deep, psychological level. Oblomov's "idealization of infantilism"[1] and refusal "to relinquish the nursery,"[2] for instance, force us to question what constitutes healthy psychological and sexual development. His slow descent into the grave, which comprises the main movement of the novel, reminds us of the great extent to which the story and its hero are haunted by the specter of death and by the threat of the abyss (*propast'* and *bezdna* in the Russian text), an image that repeats some twenty-five times throughout the book. The novel confronts us with a whole host of troubling issues that hold important insights into the nature of Goncharov's protagonist and the problems posed by his story. Among these issues are the problem of the traps and burdens of the flesh, the emptiness of human endeavor, the destructive forces of the will to power, our fear of extinction, and our social and cultural taboos about sex. Although rarely commented on and then mainly in passing, the novel's artful and often submerged treatment of these themes is powerful, compelling, and ahead of its time. It not only anticipates some of the larger questions of existentialist philosophy but, more important for this analysis, it also illustrates in almost classic fashion discoveries about the nature of the human psyche that Freud would make, some forty to fifty years after the novel's publication, in his theories on psychoanalysis. How Goncharov's psychological portrait of his neurotic slumberer coincides with the insights of Freudian psychoanalysis, and how this affects our reading of the novel, are at the center of my investigation.

Russian critics of the last century – most notably, Nikolay Dobrolyubov – saw in the novel mainly its social significance. Oblomov was "a sign of the times"; his apathy, laziness and dependence on others (his *oblomovism*) represented the ailment of the serf-owning class, which stood in the way of social reform. This view of the book and its hero, with slight adjustments to fit revolutionary mythology and minor variations in focus, prevailed throughout the Soviet period as well.[3] Even one of the novel's translators into English, David Magarshack, although acknowledging that the greatness of Oblomov "as a work of art lies in the universality of its hero," nevertheless asserts that the book is "a powerful condemnation of serfdom . . . all the more effective for being indirect and implicit."[4]

Outside of Russia, approaches to the novel have been more diverse. Many of these studies, although not overtly psychoanalytical, have suggested the appropriateness of Freud's ideas for interpreting and understanding Goncharov's hero. Besides Marc Slonim and Richard Freeborn, whose comments on Oblomov's infantile nature were cited above, some six other scholars comment on Oblomov's regressive personality in essentially Freudian terms. Leon Stilman was the first to characterize Oblomov's attraction to Agafya Matveyevna as a "regression," adding that his "death suggests return to the darkness and peace of the prenatal universe."[5] Similarly, Renato Poggioli states that to the reader "well acquainted with the concepts of depth psychology," Oblomov's relationship with Agafya Matveyevna reveals his "ever-childish urge to return to the womb."[6] Other critics make analogous comments. The Lyngstads claim that Goncharov's hero suffers from a "deep yearning to return to the womb," which represents "a death wish."[7] Kenneth Harper asserts that Oblomov "constantly searches for a mother-figure in his relations with women," a fact "consistent with his wish to return to the womb (Oblomovka)."[8] Faith Wigzell speaks of Oblomov's search for "the ideal mother," a quest she says can be characterized as "a return to the nursery."[9] In Francois de Labriolle's assessment, Oblomov's dressing gown symbolizes "the enclosed world 'par excellence' of intra-uterine life," while Oblomov himself suffers from "a weaning complex" that can only be resolved by his marriage to the "wife-mother" Agafya Matveyevna.[10] Finally, Milton Mays evokes Freud's theory of the life and death instincts from *Beyond the Pleasure Principle* (1920) in order to juxtapose Oblomov, as an embodiment of the latter instinct, with Faust, who personifies the former.[11] While offering welcome rereadings of Goncharov's work, these observations also underscore the importance and applicability of Freudian thought to a full understanding of the novel. For all their similar and valid psychoanalytical insights into the story, however, in none of these studies is a sustained Freudian analysis attempted. Indeed, in all but Labriolle's article the application of psychoanalytical concepts to Oblomov's story is done in passing, in a sentence or at most a paragraph. This outcome is unfortunate, for at best these brief assessments only scratch the surface of the complex psychological issues of Goncharov's novel. The deeper and more disturbing aspects of Oblomov's character and the complexes that surround him, Stolz and Olga, have yet to be explored in detail.

Let us take as a starting point the most oft-cited psychoanalytical interpretation mentioned above, that of Oblomov's desire to return to the womb. Reappearing consistently over the forty years during which the studies above were written, the notion that Oblomov wishes to regress to some sort of infantile state has become a commonplace in Western critiques of the novel. It is also arguably the most important psychoanalytical insight into Oblomov's personality and deserves more detailed analysis than it has been given to date. Our first clue that Oblomov might have such a regression wish comes in the first part of the novel, where we learn that he spends most of his days and nights in bed. There he escapes the pain associated with the outside world (overdue bills, the letter from his estate's bailiff, societal expectations) and gains pleasure in indolent repose and sleep. According to Freud, sleep is the psychic reenactment of prenatal life. "Our relationship with the world which we entered so unwillingly," he states, "seems to be endurable only with intermission; hence we withdraw again periodically into the condition prior to our entrance into the world: that is to say, into intra-uterine existence."[12]

Oblomov's excessive need of sleep, then, speaks to his desire to reexperience the prenatal state. Indeed, when Oblomov wants to sleep, his servant Zakhar must first effectively re-create the environment of the womb by "sealing" his master up in his room: "Zakhar began to seal up his master in the study; first he covered him up and tucked the blanket under him, then he drew the blinds, closed the door tightly, and retired to his own room."[13] Thus the enclosed space of Oblomov's bed and the "private, limited, confined world" of his bedroom are symbolic of his regression wish.[14]

Much like a baby in the womb, Oblomov only feels at home when he is in a comfortable, warm, and confined place. To cite one example, Oblomov expresses particular admiration for the lodgings of a former colleague, Ivan Gerasimovich, where the sofas are "so deep that you sink into them and can't be seen" and the windows "are covered with ivy and cactus." Ivan Gerasimovich's is a place where "you come and you don't want to go away. You sit without thinking or worrying about anything" (171).[15] So dominant is Oblomov's need of womblike confinement that even the landscape in his cherished vision of his childhood home at Oblomovka is as comfortably enclosed as a mother's womb.

The sky there seems to hug the earth, not in order to fling its thunderbolts at it, but to embrace it more tightly and lovingly; it hangs as low overhead as the trustworthy roof of the parental house, to preserve, it would seem, the chosen spot from all calamities. (104)

Given the essentially womblike features of the landscape of Oblomov's childhood home as he reconstructs it in his dream, it is not surprising that the most important figure in Oblomovka is his mother, whose appearance in his dream causes him to be "thrilled with joy" and to shed "two warm tears" (110). In Oblomov's dream, as in his childhood, his mother covers him with passionate kisses and, together with his nanny, sees to his every wish and desire.

The desire to escape to a confined and safe place and the image of the mother, then, are the essential elements of Oblomov's regression wish. His Oblomovka-ideal is the object of his dreams as an adult, which serve as a reassuring refuge from the pressing realities of the outside world. Thus his vision of his childhood home – the poetic centerpiece of the novel – not only explains his personality[16] but provides Oblomov with "a satisfaction in place of one lacking in reality," an outcome that signals the regression of his libido to a previous time of life.[17] According to Freud,

> the neurotic is in some way tied to a period in his past life; we know now that this period in the past is one in which his libido could attain satisfaction, one in which he was happy. He looks back on his life-story, seeking some such period, and goes on seeking it, even if he must go back to the time when he was a suckling infant to find it according to his recollection or his imagination of it under later influences.[18]

In Freudian psychoanalysis, this regression is achieved at great cost and brings into conflict the essential components of the human personality: the id, the ego, and the superego. The id is the seat of the "unknown and unconscious" and is the source of libidinal energy and the life and death instincts. It is ruled by the pleasure principle, which seeks to avoid or reduce pain, discomfort, or tension.[19] The ego, where perception and consciousness reside, is governed by the reality principle, which mediates between the needs of the id and the possibility, advisability, or permissibility of satisfying those needs in the real world. The ego seeks to transform "the id's will into action" while trying "to hold in check" the id's "superior strength."[20] The superego is the "ego ideal" or conscience, the source of our moral judgment and ideals.[21]

Regression violates the normal system of checks and balances by which the ego seeks to keep the id under control. The prohibited libidinal urgings of the id in regression attempt to "elude, eschew the ego. . . . [T]he libido withdraws itself from the ego and its laws" seeking the fixations needed to break through the ego's repressions, according to Freud, in "the activities and experiences of infantile sexuality" and "the component tendencies and the objects of childhood which have been relinquished and abandoned. It is to them, therefore, that the libido turns back."[22] The most important figure in both infantile and adult sexuality, Freud argues, is that of the mother.

> A child's first erotic object is the mother's breast that nourishes it. . . . This first object is later completed into the person of the child's mother, who not only nourishes it but also looks after it and thus arouses in it a number of other physical sensations, pleasurable and unpleasurable. By her care of the child's body she becomes its first seducer. In these two relations lies the root of a mother's importance, unique, without parallel, established unalterably for a whole lifetime as the first and strongest love-object and as the prototype of all later love relations – for both sexes.[23]

For Oblomov, the mother who smothered him with passionate kisses and the nanny who acts as a mother substitute fulfill this function. Indeed, their features are discernible in the two relationships Oblomov has with Olga Sergeyevna and Agafya Matveyevna, and it is these two relationships that ultimately reveal the Oedipal nature of Oblomov's regression wish. Both Olga Sergeyevna and Agafya Matveyevna are mother figures for Oblomov. Olga is most like Oblomov's mother and wife ideal; Agafya Matveyevna fulfills the function of his former nanny in her role as caretaker and also plays the part of the seductive peasant girl from Oblomov's sensual daydreams. Both also complement Oblomov's id-driven personality as ego-agents of a sort who curb his primal urges, Olga by trying to reform his indulgent ways, Agafya by trying to satisfy them. Olga is primarily linked to Oblomov's mother through their mutual association with lilac blooms. In Oblomov's dream we learn that the scent of lilac poured in through the windows of his mother's bedroom (110), and later in the novel a sprig of lilac comes to symbolize the short-lived romance between Olga and Oblomov.[24] Elsewhere, the placid, passionless figure of Oblomov's mother reappears in one of his daydreams about his ideal wife (who is the embodiment of "grave repose" and "the personification of rest itself" [202]) only to be superimposed on the image of Olga herself in other daydreams in which Olga is the "divine angel" in the "earthly paradise" of Oblomovka who joins him in the "gentle flow" of life in the country (215) or walks "dreamily" around the grounds with him (271). The specter of the mother figure is later raised once more in a conversation between Olga and Oblomov about their relationship. After forcing a declaration of love out of him, Olga then refuses to say she is likewise in love with him: "'In love – no, I don't like that expression: I love you!'" Oblomov retorts: "'But one may love one's mother, father, nurse, and even one's dog: all this is covered by the general, collective term "I love."' . . . One does not fall in love with one's father, mother, or nurse, but loves them'" (239). Or does one? The implication Oblomov raises is intriguing, as is Olga's refusal to clarify the issue. Oblomov himself seems to be hinting at the cultural taboos surrounding the Oedipus complex, even as he gives his own Oedipus complex expression in his attraction to Olga.

Olga's relationship with Oblomov, in which she places prohibitions on him, sets rules for him, and gives him tasks, is essentially that of a parent. She continually manifests "her despotic will over him," asking him "not only what he had been doing, but also what he was going to do" and making him "tremble" under her glance when he fails to fulfill her tasks (238–39). At the same time she keeps watch over him "like a guardian angel" (263). She is his "Casta Diva," his chaste goddess, but like the subject of the aria Oblomov admires so much, or like any virginal goddess for that matter, she is inaccessible to his Oedipal urges for a variety of reasons.[25] In part, Olga's inaccessibility lies in her greater distance from him as an ideal (rather than real) mother/wife object, hence his characterization of her as an angel in his famous letter to her (246–49) and her "divine" nature in his earlier daydreams of her (81, 215).[26] This distance causes, in Oblomov's words, an "abyss" to open up between them.

This abyss, according to Richard Peace, is that of passion and "may be traced back to the ravine in Oblomovka,"[27] a place that Milton Ehre identifies as "a symbol of all that is forbidden, for the smell of death is there."[28] The two images are clearly linked, for both the ravine of his childhood and the abyss of his adult years demarcate forbidden territory for Oblomov. In a Freudian reading, this forbidden territory is the abyss of forbidden incestuous love. The recesses of this abyss are those of the womb to which Oblomov wishes to return, and the abyss itself ultimately becomes the grave that Oblomov prepares for himself at the end of the book as the consequence of his attraction to the forbidden mother object.[29] Nathalie Baratoff, in her Jungian reading of the novel, likens the "shape of the ravine" to "the female genitalia," an analogy that explains "the great prohibition of approaching it, as well as the young boy's fascination and fear of it," associations all bound up with "chthonic sexuality."[30] In his letter to Olga, Oblomov hints at the dangerous nature of his abyss at whose bottom he is lying. He mentions the word *abyss* three times and cautions her from looking down into it when she is "soaring high above it like a pure angel" (247). Nevertheless Olga talks him out of his fears, rejecting his letter as a cruel trick. In dismissing his fears of the abyss,[31] she also essentially reinvites his Oedipal attentions.

So what makes Oblomov eventually reject Olga? And why does Oblomov withdraw from her at all when he is quite content to resign himself to the abyss of forbidden love with his other mother object, Agafya Matveyevna? The answer, I believe, has to do with one of the most famous (and least talked about) sex scenes in Russian literature: that of Olga's orgasm in the garden.[32]

Freud posits castration anxiety as the antidote to the Oedipus complex. The threat of the removal of the offending organ is supposed to shock the male out of his desire to sleep with his mother, especially if the threat is accompanied by a reminder that women lack a penis. The entire process, according to Freud, is "the greatest problem of early life and the strongest source of later inadequacy" in men.[33] For Oblomov, this experience is reenacted one sultry night on a walk with Olga. It is dark, the landscape is decidedly Freudian: "The trees and bushes were merged into a gloomy mass; one could not see two paces ahead; only the winding, sandy paths showed white. . . . [T]hey groped their way down a narrow avenue between two black, impenetrable walls of trees" (265).

Olga is afraid with a "delightful fear"; she trembles, whispers rapturously, and clutches at Oblomov, all the while breathing hotly and irregularly. They sit on a bench and she squeezes his hand, burning inside and speaking languidly and inaudibly. Oblomov listens to her heavy breathing in the darkness, feels her warm tears on his hand and the convulsive pressure of her fingers and all the while begs her to let him take her back to the house. He is anxious and alarmed. When her "lunatism of love"[34] passes, they walk back to the house. She is unsteady on her feet and gazes at Oblomov in parting with "a look of exhaustion in her face" and an "ardent smile." "He had seen that smile somewhere: he remembered a picture of a woman with such a smile – only it was not Cordelia" (267). In other words, it is not the smile of King Lear's daughter, who loves out of duty. Olga's smile is one of consummation.[35]

The irony, of course, is that Oblomov plays an all but superfluous role in this "consummation" of their relationship. Olga's orgasm, achieved on a highly symbolic walk through a sexually suggestive landscape, is accomplished without recourse to Oblomov's penis. Dominant in all other aspects of their relationship, Olga through her orgasm symbolically deprives Oblomov of his last sign of masculinity and lays bare the castration anxiety latent in any Oedipal relationship. Indeed, as if to compensate for his resultant feeling of inadequacy and to counteract Olga's threatening sexuality, Oblomov later accuses himself of being "a seducer, a lady-killer" (271), thereby lessening the castration anxiety he feels by transferring the aggressive sexual role to himself in his relationship with Olga. In this new role, Oblomov goes so far as to propose marriage. But Olga remains too remote and too dangerous for Oblomov to carry through with his Oedipal wish.[36] Certainly the match would never have been allowed to proceed once Stolz – the father figure in this triangle – found out, as we can deduce by his reaction on finding out of Olga's and Oblomov's relationship later in the novel: "'Oblomov! . . . It's impossible! . . . There's something wrong here: you did not understand yourself, Oblomov, or love!'" (408).[37] Significantly, no sooner is Oblomov's proposal made than Olga is supplanted by another, less threatening mother object, Agafya Matveyevna.[38]

Like Olga, Agafya is also prefigured in Oblomov's daydreams, but whereas Olga assumed the image and likeness of the mother/wife ideal, Agafya is first glimpsed as the "rosy-cheeked maid-servant with soft, round bare arms and a sunburnt neck" who brings Oblomov his meals in one fantasy (82) and who, in another, "pretends to avoid her master's caress" (179). This image of the slyly sensual provider is confirmed when Oblomov first catches sight of Agafya, "a rather plump woman, with a bare neck and elbows and no cap on, who smiled at having been seen by a stranger" (291). From then on, Agafya is metonymically identified by her bare neck and arms, busily moving elbows, and her bosom, high and "firm as a sofa cushion" (293). All told, some forty such metonymic references are made to Agafya, whose moving elbows, bare neck, bare arms, bare shoulders, and well-developed bosom describe a very important anatomical inventory whose sum is far greater than its parts. Agafya Matveyevna becomes for both Oblomov and the reader that part of the mother's anatomy from which nourishment and sensual pleasure is first derived, the place between the crook of the elbows cradling the child and holding it to the exposed breast that feeds it and the bare arms and shoulders that form the borders of the baby's world during feeding. It is in this way that the narration gives us Oblomov's "baby's-eye" view of the world, explaining as well, perhaps, why

Oblomov's servant Anisya likewise becomes metonymically identified as a talking nose some nine times in the novel, beginning,
significantly, after Oblomov moves to Agafya's rooms in Vyborg.

By virtue of her simple, lower-class origins, Agafya is most like
Oblomov's nanny, who, unlike his mother, was actually the one who
nursed, bathed, and dressed him and saw to his needs throughout the
day. Agafya is the true object of Oblomov's regression wish, for she
alone, as his nanny surrogate, can undo "the traumatic experience of
weaning"[39] and satisfy his needs – libidinal and otherwise – according to the pleasure principle, which governs his id-driven existence
just as it did the mythical world of the Oblomovka he reconstructs
from his childhood. His dream of Oblomovka, of course, was the
source of his regression wish in the first place.

Agafya is the ultimate provider, of food mainly but also of sexual
excitement.[40] In Oblomov's life the two are clearly linked, just as
they are for the infant, for whom food and sexual pleasure are bound
up in the image of the mother's breast. Agafya Matveyevna, whose
bare arms constantly thrust pies and vodka through the door of the
kitchen (300, 310, 367), is at once a provider of food and a sensual
object. At one point Oblomov looks at her "with the same pleasure
with which he had looked at her hot cheese-cakes that morning"
(331). Elsewhere, he derives pleasure from glimpsing her busy elbows at work in the kitchen.[41] Indeed, "all he wanted was to sit on
the sofa without taking his eyes off her elbows" (379). Those very
same elbows are a distinct source of arousal for Oblomov, who playfully grabs hold of them when he kisses the nape of Agafya's neck.
Indeed, after this first kiss, Agafya finds a suspicious oily stain on the
skirt of Oblomov's dressing-gown (which he had resumed wearing in
her house). The stain is apparently not the first that Agafya reports
finding, and although she suggests oil from the icon lamp or grease
from the door hinges as possible causes, the incidents seem to point
as well to the "amplified auto-erotism" Freud says accompanies the
regressive libido. According to Freud, "amplified auto-erotism . . .
offered the sexual instinct its first gratifications"; its reemergence is a
consequence of the regressive neurotic's rejection of the reality prin-

ciple for the pleasure principle.[42] Oblomov's own explanation of the stain is decidedly vague: "I'm afraid I don't know where I can have acquired it," he states, after which he gazes at Agafya "with mild excitement" (378–79). Throughout parts 3 and 4 of the novel, food and sex, onanism and intercourse, are often blurred in Oblomov's relationship with Agafya.

Unlike Olga, whose relationship with Oblomov was driven by the restrictive dictums of the reality principle, Agafya Matveyevna indulges his every desire, most particularly, his Oedipal desire to sleep with his mother. For one thing, she is, conveniently enough, a widow, so there is no prohibiting, punishing father to thwart Oblomov's Oedipal wish. There is a father figure, Agafya's brother Ivan Matveyevich, who has phallic red, thick, slightly shaking fingers which he believed "with good reason" were "not quite nice to display . . . too often" (301).[43] But far from thwarting Oblomov's Oedipal wish as the castrating father, Ivan Matveyevich actually aids and abets it in his desire to swindle Oblomov out of thousands of rubles. He even moves out of Agafya's house at one point as if to remove the threatening father figure as far away as possible (418). Everything seems to come together to provide the right environment in which Oblomov can complete his regression and fulfill his Oedipal wish.

The final impediment comes from Oblomov's childhood friend Stolz, who visits Oblomov at his Vyborg lodgings and, sensing Oblomov's illicit relationship with Agafya, warns him "not to fall into the pit" (437).[44] Stolz, who constantly appeals to noble aspirations and ideals in his attempt to rouse Oblomov out of his sleepy life,[45] introduces a moral imperative into his friend's life, playing in this regard something akin to the role of the superego to Oblomov's id personification and the ego incarnations of Olga and Agafya. In this way we can say that Stolz symbolically completes the collective human personality Goncharov seems to be investigating in his novel. Certainly as moral and idealistic guide to Oblomov, teacher and mentor to Olga, and champion of justice to Agafya,[46] Stolz is a perfect embodiment of the superego even as he is too good to be true and the least lifelike of any of the characters in the book.[47] Stolz

immediately senses the immoral nature of Oblomov's relationship
with Agafya (436). Indeed, he seems fully aware of Oblomov's perverse regression wish, and vows to take him "out of this pit, this bog,
into the light, into the open, *to a healthy, normal life!*" (474–75; my
emphasis).[48] But he is unsuccessful. Stolz is not the prohibitive father figure in this relationship – that role is restricted to the
Oblomov-Olga-Stolz triangle. Oblomov is free to indulge his Oedipal desire. Indeed, both friends sense the consequences, embracing
in parting "as people embrace . . . before death" (475). Oblomov, it
seems, is doomed.

Oblomov's regression is complete. He marries the forbidden
mother and has a child by her as he begins his slow descent into a
vegetative, womblike existence in the Vyborg house under Agafya's
motherly care.[49] Though it is "shorn of poetry and bereft of the
brilliance with which his imagination" had once endowed his dream
of Oblomovka (465), Oblomov finds his life at Agafya's house to be
proof that "the ideally reposeful aspect of human existence" is possible (466). Death catches him unawares, in his sleep.

It is a central paradox of the novel that Oblomov's vision of life
and his premature demise (he is only in his forties when he dies) are
not provided a more compelling "positive" alternative. Indeed, the
relationship between Stolz and Olga – clearly meant to be an ideal of
sorts – and their philosophy of life are plagued by their inability to
divine any better answer to the big questions of life and death than
those proposed by Oblomov in his vision of Oblomovka. Everything
about their life is just "as Oblomov dreamed" (445), an outcome that
torments Olga, who is deathly afraid of sinking into "an apathy like
Oblomov's" (448). Stolz tells her that this is the price we "pay for the
Promethean fire," for the knowledge that all striving ends in death,
knowledge that brings us "to the abyss from which we can get no
answer" (453). It is, he says, the "general ailment of mankind" (454).
But, while Olga and Stolz ostensibly seek their answer in each other
and in the family they raise, the "ailment" to which they refer is
essentially that of the curse of being born, whose origins and ulti-

mate answer lie with the mother. Indeed, early in their relationship, each of them sees a mother figure of sorts in the other.

When they meet in Switzerland, Olga looks at Stolz "as she would not look at anyone, except perhaps at her mother, if she had a mother" (396). Later she tells him that she trusts him "entirely, as my mother" (407), and elsewhere she puts her head on his chest "as though he were her mother" (415). For his part, Stolz associates Olga's tender voice with the memory of his mother's fragrant room (415) and harbors a "dream of a mother who created and took part in the social and spiritual life of a whole generation of happy people," a dream he hopes Olga will fulfill for him (447). It is as though Olga is in search of a mother substitute for the one she never knew, and Stolz seeks to replace the one who died in his childhood (159), the mother who compensated for his father's austere German manners with Russian "softness, delicacy" and "true understanding" (155). In essence, Olga's and Stolz's ailment is, like Oblomov's, also bound up in a search for the mother, whose presence brings meaning to life.

The image of the mother, of course, has a variety of possible connotations and associations, many of them life-affirming and positive. Jung, for instance, says the mother is "the accidental carrier of that great experience which includes herself and myself and all mankind, and indeed the whole of created nature, the experience of life whose children we are." For Jung, "mother love" is "one of the most moving and unforgettable memories of our lives, the mysterious root of all growth and change; the love that means homecoming, shelter, and the long silence from which everything begins and in which everything ends."[50] But even Jung devotes considerable analysis to the negative effects of a variety of mother complexes,[51] and Freud, as we have seen, attaches all sorts of prohibitions to the figure of the mother. As Marianne Hirsch says, "for psychoanalysis, and in a large part even for psychoanalytic feminism, a continued allegiance to the mother appears as regressive and potentially lethal; it must be transcended. Maturity can be reached only through an alignment with the paternal, by means of an angry and hostile break from the mother."[52] In the novel Oblomov, Olga, and Stolz cannot seem to make that break, and they suffer for it. Oblomov's is by far the worst failure in this regard. But even Olga and Stolz fail, and their constant interest in and reminiscences of their friend only underscore their similar situations and fates.

While Jung posits as the three essential aspects of the mother "her cherishing and nourishing goodness, her orgiastic emotionality, and her Stygian depths,"[53] it is the latter image that haunts the novel. The novel is replete with references to death, from Zakhar's refrain "I wish I were dead!" repeated some five times in part 1 to the more than dozen images of death and dying in Oblomov's dream. In part 2 death, speculation of death, and threats of dying accompany the development of the romance between Olga and Oblomov.[54] In part 3 Oblomov swears he will die without Olga (345), only to be told later by Olga that he "died long ago" and is "dead" now (362). Part 4 chronicles Oblomov's settling into his "plain and spacious coffin" (466), an image reinforced in Stolz's last meeting with Oblomov, in which death and dying are mentioned a half dozen times. Add to this the recurring image of the abyss and we can see that the novel is permeated by the spirit of collapse, decay, and extinction, which are the disturbing associations with which we leave the novel.[55]

In the end the collision between eros and destruction, between Freud's life and death instincts, is played out in the novel deep within the component parts of the human personality. Indeed, the broad appeal of the novel lies in part in its subtle evocation of the complicated issues of the human psyche and human sexuality. V. S. Pritchett calls Oblomov one of the "'great' or outsize characters in fiction" who are "the revenges of the unconscious."[56] Goncharov himself admitted that his writing belonged in the category of "unconscious creativity" (*bessoznatel'noe tvorchestvo*).[57] To what extent he invested in his hero aspects of his own unconscious personality is unknown, although Pritchett claims that the death of Goncharov's father when the writer was only four years old is "an accident of personal life to be taken into account. . . . [L]ike Oblomov himself, [Goncharov] longed for the rest and passive pleasure of lying in a mother's arms."[58] The Lyngstads note the "striking similarity between Agafya Matveevna's name and patronymic, and those of Goncharov's own mother, Avdotya Matveevna."[59] It seems unwise and unnecessary, however, to speculate whether Goncharov was attempting some sort of psycho-autobiography in his novel. The aspects of the unconscious that Oblomov explores, after all, are of a universal nature. What is more interesting and perhaps more productive is to speculate how the questions Goncharov's book raises about our relation to the unconscious change the way we read the novel. Freudian theory offers one important starting place for such a rereading.

NOTES

1. Marc Slonim, *The Epic of Russian Literature* (New York: Oxford University Press, 1964), p. 187.

2. Richard Freeborn, *The Rise of the Russian Novel: Studies in the Russian Novel from Eugene Onegin to War and Peace* (London: Cambridge University Press, 1973), p. 150.

3. Typical in this regard is the afterword to the 1954 Children's Literature publication of the novel, which states: "The main thing in the novel *Oblomov* is its ideological orientation against serfdom, its unmasking of the social system founded on slavery and the oppression of the people" (A. Kotov, "O romane I. A. Goncharova 'Oblomov,'" in I. A. Goncharov, *Oblomov* [Moscow: Detskaia literatura, 1954], p. 528).

4. David Magarshack, "Introduction," in Ivan Goncharov, *Oblomov*, trans. David Magarshack (London: Penguin, 1954), p. vii.

5. Leon Stilman, "Oblomovka Revisited," *The American Slavic and East European Review* 7 (1948): 68.

6. Renato Poggioli, *The Phoenix and the Spider* (Cambridge: Harvard University Press, 1957), p. 43.

7. Alexandra Lyngstad and Sverre Lyngstad, *Ivan Goncharov* (New York: Twayne, 1971), pp. 96–97.

8. Kenneth E. Harper, "Under the Influence of Oblomov," *From Los Angeles to Kiev: Papers on the Occasion of the Ninth International Congress of Slavists, Kiev, September 1983*, ed. Vladimir Markov and Dean S. Worth (Columbus, Ohio: Slavica, 1983), p. 116.

9. Faith Wigzell, "Dream and Fantasy in Goncharov's *Oblomov*," *From Pushkin to Palisandriia: Essays on the Russian Novel in Honor of Richard Freeborn*, ed. Arnold McMillin (New York: St. Martin's, 1990), p. 101.

10. Francois de Labriolle, "Oblomov n'est-il qu'un paresseux?" *Cahiers du monde russe et sovietique* 10.1 (1969): 48, 50.

11. Milton A. Mays, "Oblomov as Anti-Faust," *Western Humanities Review* 21 (1967): 152.

12. Sigmund Freud, *A General Introduction to Psychoanalysis*, trans. Joan Riviere (New York: Pocket, 1971), p. 92.

13. Ivan Goncharov, *Oblomov*, trans. David Magarshack, p. 99. All references to this edition will be given parenthetically in the text.

14. Labriolle, "Oblomov n'est-il qu'un paresseux?" p. 48.

15. Labriolle cites this passage as well but mistakenly asserts that this is Oblomov's characterization of Agafya Matveyevna's rooms (see ibid.).

16. Its chief function, according to the Lyngstads. See their *Ivan Goncharov*, p. 79.

17. Freud, *Introduction*, p. 374.

18. Ibid.

19. Sigmund Freud, *The Ego and the Id*, trans. Joan Riviere, rev. and ed. James Strachey (New York: W. W. Norton, 1960), pp. 17, 19, 45.

20. Ibid., pp. 19–20.

21. Ibid., pp. 23, 30–33.

22. Freud, *Introduction*, pp. 368–70.

23. Sigmund Freud, *An Outline of Psycho-Analysis*, trans. and ed. James Strachey (New York: W. W. Norton, 1949), p. 70.

24. The sprig of lilac that Olga tears off and then throws down in vexation in chapter 6 of part 2 only to be picked up by Oblomov in chapter 7 comes to symbolize their relationship, which blooms, then withers and dies. For more on the significance of the lilac imagery, see Richard Peace, *Oblomov: A Critical Examination of Goncharov's Novel* (Birmingham: University of Birmingham Press, 1991), pp. 41–46; Milton Ehre, *Oblomov and His Creator: The Life and Art of Ivan Goncharov* (Princeton, N.J.: Princeton University Press, 1973), pp. 182–95. See also Galya Diment, "The Precocious Talent of Ivan Goncharov," and Karl D. Kramer, "Mistaken Identities and Compatible Couples in *Oblomov*," both in this volume.

25. For more on the aria, see Karl D. Kramer, "Mistaken Identities and Compatible Couples in *Oblomov*," in this volume.

26. Relevant in this regard is the time Olga refuses to give Oblomov a kiss, becoming in her indignation "an offended goddess of pride and anger with compressed lips and lightning in her eyes" (259).

27. Peace, *Oblomov*, p. 71.

28. Ehre, *Oblomov and His Creator*, p. 177.

29. Oblomov's marriage to Agafya Matveyevna signals his doom; his life with her becomes a rehearsal for his impending death: "As years passed, he was less and less disturbed by remorse and agitation, and settled quietly and gradually into the plain and spacious coffin he had made for his remaining span of life, like old hermits who, turning away from life, dig their own graves in the desert" (466).

30. Nathalie Baratoff, *Oblomov: A Jungian Approach. A Literary Image of the Mother Complex* (Bern: Peter Lang, 1990), p. 48.

31. At one point Olga even taunts Oblomov's fear that an abyss will open at their feet, saying to him: "'Well, what of it? Let it!'" (276).

32. Nikita Mikhalkov seems to agree with this interpretation. In his 1980 screen adaptation of the novel, *Several Days in the Life of I. I. Oblomov*, Olga's "lunatism of love" (superbly rendered by actress Elena Solovei) is obviously an orgasm, the more remarkable for its surviving the cuts of prudish Soviet movie censors.

33. Freud, *Outline*, p. 74.

34. "Lunatizm liubvi," translated by Magarshack as "somnambulism of love" (265).

35. The Lyngstads call the scene "clearly sexual in origin" but do not expound on its meaning except to say that it speaks to "a deep erotic frustration" on Olga's part that continues in her marriage to Stolz (Ivan Goncharov, *Oblomov*, pp. 103–4). Peace describes Olga's "fit" in some detail and states that she "significantly" omits mention of it when she tells Stolz about her relationship with Oblomov, but he does not explain what her fit is or why it is important that Olga should be self-conscious about it later (Peace, *Oblomov*, pp. 51–52). I argue that her self-consciousness is strong indication that she did indeed have a sexual "encounter" with Oblomov in the garden, even if it was somewhat one-sided.

36. Baratoff argues that although Oblomov's libido is "stuck in the mother," it is not a real mother he seeks, but the Great Mother – the abstract mother ideal of the mother complex: "It is the unconscious which provides the man with a mother complex with images of such captivating

richness and vividness that no real woman can compete for long. As in Oblomov's case, the woman outside is idealized because feared, and feared perhaps rightly, for she is potentially the one to break the man's bond to the Great Mother" (see her *Oblomov: A Jungian Approach*, p. 49).

37. See, also, Stolz's thoughts after "several years": "He was horror-stricken only when he remembered that Olga had been within a hair's breadth of destruction; that they had merely stumbled on their right path in life, and their two lives, now merged into one, might have diverged; that ignorance of the ways of life might have led to a disastrous mistake, that Oblomov – He shuddered" (457).

38. Goncharov places the highly significant break between parts 2 and 3 of the novel just after the marriage proposal and just before Oblomov first meets Agafya Matveyevna.

39. Freud, *Introduction*, p. 375.

40. For an expanded treatment of food in Oblomov, see Ronald D. LeBlanc, "Oblomov's Consuming Passion: Food, Eating, and the Search for Communion," in this volume.

41. Goncharov, *Oblomov*, trans. David Magarshack, pp. 309, 313, 329, 334, 377.

42. Freud, *Introduction*, p. 375.

43. Ivan Matveyevich's phallic fingers are also mentioned on pages 352 and 355.

44. Although Stolz uses the words *pit* (*iama*) and *bog* (*boloto*) to describe the threatening place that Oblomov must avoid, his use of these terms essentially evokes the same images of unhealthy sensuality and illicit sexuality as that of Oblomov's *bezdna* and *propast'*. In any case, a pit or bog are certainly earthly equivalents of an abyss.

45. See, in particular, chapter 4 of part 2, especially pages 181–83.

46. It is Stolz who discovers and confounds the swindle attempted by Agafya's brother, thus most certainly saving her (and Oblomov's) life. See chapter 7, part 4.

47. This outcome is entirely to be expected from a character who is supposed to represent the ideal, as opposed to the real.

48. The Russian is "Von iz etoi iamy, iz bolota, na svet, na prostor, gde est' zdorovaia, normal'naia zhizn'!" Magarshack's translation omits "zdorovaia" (healthy).

49. It is significant in this regard that the rooms of Agafya's house are

small and have low ceilings, about which Olga complains on her visit there to see Oblomov (343).

50. C. G. Jung, *Four Archetypes: Mother, Rebirth, Spirit, Trickster*, trans. R.F.C. Hull (Princeton, N.J.: Princeton University Press, 1969), p. 26.

51. See Jung, *Four Archetypes*, pp. 19–25, 32–44.

52. Marianne Hirsch, *The Mother/Daughter Plot: Narrative, Psychoanalysis, Feminism* (Bloomington: Indiana University Press, 1989), p. 168.

53. Jung, *Four Archetypes*, p. 16.

54. Goncharov, *Oblomov*, trans. David Magarshack, pp. 240, 253, 257, 273, 278.

55. Baratoff's Jungian analysis comes to an opposite conclusion. She argues that Jung's rereading of Freud's sexual theory indicates "that the incest wish need not necessarily be taken concretely, but may be seen symbolically as a reentry into the unconscious (the mother) with the expectation of rebirth." This rebirth is figured in the birth of Oblomov's son, Andrey. See her *Oblomov: A Jungian Approach*, p. 107. Mikhalkov's film points to a similar interpretation by making a link between Oblomov as a child in the film's opening and little Andrey in the film's conclusion. Both cry out joyfully at the news of their mother's arrival: "Mamin'ka priekhala!" (Mommie's come!).

56. V. S. Pritchett, Untitled rev. of Ivan Goncharov, *Oblomov*, trans. David Magarshack, *The New Statesman and Nation* (20 November 1954): 661.

57. I. A. Goncharov, "Luchshe pozdno chem nikogda," in his *Sobranie sochinenii* (Moscow: Pravda, 1954), vol. 8, p. 69.

58. Pritchett, Untitled rev. Harry T. Moore states outright that for Goncharov "Oblomov was largely a self-portrait" ("Foreword" Ivan Goncharov, *Oblomov*, trans. Ann Dunnigan (New York: Signet, 1963), p. xiii.

59. Lyngstad and Lyngstad, *Ivan Goncharov*, p. 171 n. 13. They also note the similarity between Oblomov's relationship with Agafya and "the connection between the gentleman N. N. Tregubov and Mrs. Goncharov. . . . Tregubov for many years had a common household with Goncharov's mother."

Oblomov's Consuming Passion: Food, Eating, and the Search for Communion

RONALD D. LEBLANC

Although Ilya Ilyich himself might well insist that his romantic love for Olga Ilyinskaya is the passion that threatens to "consume" him, readers of Goncharov's famous novel are more likely to contend that it is Oblomov's great love of food and eating that instead constitutes the hero's true "consuming" passion. Food imagery and depictions of scenes of eating obviously play a prominent part in "Oblomov's Dream" (part 1, chapter 9), of course, where the narrator relates the hero's nostalgic vision of his childhood spent on the idyllic ancestral estate at Oblomovka. But gastronomic motifs likewise dominate parts 3 and 4 of the novel, as we watch the indolent Oblomov become slowly seduced by the domestic routines and culinary rhythms of Agafya Matveyevna's household in the Vyborg district of St. Petersburg. For those who follow the lead of Nikolay Dobrolyubov and consider the "Oblomovitis" of Goncharov's hero primarily as a sociological and moral ailment that results from the institution of serfdom, Oblomov's extreme fondness for food and drink can be seen as emblematic of the indolence, lethargy, and egoism endemic to the pampered members of Russia's parasitic and exploitative gentry class. Eating seems to rank second only to sleeping as the favorite activity enjoyed by the somnolent Oblomov; in fact dining contributes directly to the hero's chronic drowsiness, since consuming a meal of heavy foods invariably brings about in him – as it did for the inhabitants of his native Oblomovka – a state of postprandial lethargy and the desire to nap. As one critic has noted, the only kind of labor performed within the Oblomovka world of complete inactivity involves either the preparation or the consumption of food.[1] It seems only fitting, therefore, that Oblomov's early death should result – as his doctor had warned – from him "lying about and eating heavy, fatty food" (87).[2] For those readers and critics who tend to understand the portrayal of Goncharov's sleepy hero mainly in psychological or even archetypal terms, however, the food imagery in *Oblomov* can be seen to function in more symbolic ways, helping not only to chart the trajectory of the romance plot in the novel, but also to define more clearly for us the hero's true identity and the more universal nature of his quest.

Although gastronomical motifs abound on an almost unprecedented scale in *Oblomov*, Goncharov's novel is by no means the first food-filled book to be written in the modern period; indeed, there is a long tradition, in Russia as well as in the West, of literary works depicting human beings in the act of satisfying their most basic biological need. The use of food imagery in Western literature, Mikhail Bakhtin argues in his pioneering study of Rabelais and medieval folk culture, initially celebrated the human body and what he calls the "material bodily principle" in a very positive and life-affirming way. "Eating and drinking," Bakhtin writes,

are one of the most significant manifestations of the grotesque body. The distinctive character of this body is its open unfinished nature, its interaction with the world. These traits are most fully and concretely revealed in the act of eating; the body transgresses here its own limits: it swallows, devours, rends the world apart, is enriched and grows at the world's expense. The encounter of man with the world, which takes place inside the open, biting, rending, chewing mouth, is one of the most ancient, and most important objects of human thought and imagery. Here man tastes the world, introduces it into his body, makes it part of himself. . . . Man's encounter with the world in the act of eating is joyful, triumphant; he triumphs over the world, devours it without being devoured himself.[3]

During the Enlightenment, however, when serious literature increasingly severs its ties with folk culture, this joyous celebration of ingestion and human corporeality gives way increasingly to satiric representations where eating is associated with the sin of gluttony and where the materiality of the body is looked down on as something inherently base and demeaning. Under the aesthetic principles of neoclassicism, the pictures of eating and drinking as joyous, celebratory, and triumphant activities provided in the works of Rabelais and other creators of carnivalized literature tend to disappear from the artistic landscape, having become, in essence, a forbidden topos. By the time Ivan Goncharov appeared on the literary scene during the middle of the nineteenth century, however, these lingering aesthetic taboos against literary representations of food, drink, and the human body had been effectively shattered by Russian prose writers – such as Alexander Izmailov, Vasily Narezhny, and Nikolay Gogol – whose so-called Flemish tendencies were evident in the colorful scenes they painted of everyday life among the common people.[4] In the wake of the groundbreaking prose fiction written by members of the Natural school, literary realists in mid-nineteenth-century Russia were able to use food imagery and fictional meals in their works in less Rabelaisian and more mimetically purposeful ways: that is, as metonyms or synecdoches through which to describe contemporary social reality. Like many of their French contemporaries – such as Balzac, Hugo, and Flaubert – nineteenth-century Russian novelists during the Age of Realism began to exploit food imagery very effectively as a narrative device for illustrating the social, economic, and political relations in their country.[5]

In *Oblomov*, one mimetic function of food imagery is to serve as a barometer of economic well-being, indicating a person's relative position on the scale between the polarities of wealth and poverty. Early in the novel, for instance, when the hero is still residing in his seedy Gorokhovaia Street apartment, the reader's impression that Oblomov has indeed fallen on hard times financially is reinforced by the comment made by his visitor, Tarantyev, that the food served at Oblomov's flat is quite wretched (46). In fact Tarantyev tries to induce Oblomov to move to the Vyborg district in part by pointing out to him that the food served at Agafya Matveyevna's household will be twice as good as the trash he is currently eating (49). In part 4, by which time Oblomov has become comfortably ensconced in his new Vyborg quarters, Goncharov again uses food imagery to help indicate the hero's deteriorating economic situation brought about by the fraudulent schemes devised against him by Tarantyev and the landlady's brother, Ivan Matveyevich Mukhoyarov. The reader is now informed that Agafya Matveyevna "did little pounding, grating, and sieving, because they could afford but little coffee, cinnamon, and almonds" (437). "She had more often nowadays to chop onions, grate horseradish, and similar condiments," he explains (437). Oblomov, we are told, had not tasted such favorite food items as cinnamon, vanilla, or thick cream for well over a year "because his coffee was not bought in pounds from the best shops, but for ten kopecks in the little shop around the corner; because his cream was not brought by a Finnish woman, but was supplied by the same little shop; because instead of a juicy chop, she was bringing him an omelette for lunch, fried with a tough piece of ham that had grown stale in the same little shop" (437). The plentiful provisions that had once characterized Agafya Matveyevna's well-stocked kitchen and larder have now all but disappeared: "sturgeon, snow-white veal, and turkeys made their appearance in another kitchen, in Ivan Matveyevich's new apartment" (438). For one of the few times in the novel, the reader is here allowed to glimpse momentarily the thoughts of Agafya Matveyevna, who muses, "How can a gentleman like him suddenly start eating buttered turnips instead of asparagus, mutton instead of hazel-grouse, salted pike-perch, and, perhaps, jelled fish from the little shop instead of Gatchina trout and high-quality sturgeon marbled with amber-colored fat?" (440).

Agafya Matveyevna resorts to pawning the pearls her late husband had once given her and to suffering privations quietly herself in order to continue feeding her beloved Oblomov the asparagus, hazel-grouse, and French peas he likes so much: "The next day Oblomov, without suspecting anything, drank the currant vodka, following it up by some excellent smoked salmon, his favorite dish of giblets, and a fresh white hazel-grouse. Agafya Matveyevna and the children had the servants' cabbage soup and porridge, and it was only to keep Oblomov company that she drank two cups of coffee" (440). This ruse does not work for long, however. When Stolz suddenly arrives back in St. Petersburg unannounced and shows up at Oblomov's for dinner, Agafya Matveyevna has neither the time nor the money to prepare a different meal for this unexpected guest. "He'll have to be satisfied with what we have," she informs Oblomov (443). It does not take Stolz long to see that the inelegant fare he is being served that evening pales in comparison to the sumptuous feast he had enjoyed there just a year earlier:

> He remembered Oblomov's name-day party: the oysters, the pineapples, the great snipe; now he saw a coarse tablecloth, cruet-bottles for oil and vinegar stopped with bits of paper instead of corks, forks with broken handles, a large round of black bread on each of their plates. Oblomov had fish soup and he had barley soup and boiled chicken, followed by mutton, then tough tongue. Red wine was served. Stolz poured himself out half a glass, had a sip, put the glass back on the table, and did not touch it again. Oblomov drank two glasses of currant vodka, one after the other, and greedily attacked the mutton. (447–48)

The pensive Stolz, we are told, "did not eat the mutton or the curd dumplings; he put down his fork and watched with what appetite Oblomov ate it all" (448). Very quickly it occurs to Stolz why it is that his corpulent friend is dining on such plain and coarse fare: "Aha! So that's the meaning of the mutton and sour wine! You have no money!" (449).

The meaning of the mutton and sour wine that Oblomov is consuming so greedily here resides in their significance not only as indicators of socioeconomic well-being but also as symbols of the disputed national identity: that is, the conflict between the native and the foreign, of Russia and the West. What Lynn Visson calls a "gastronomic dialectic" between Slavophilism and Westernism is at work throughout nineteenth-century Russian literature and culture, where the simple, hearty, native cooking of the peasantry is often pitted against the more elegant and sophisticated cuisine that the Europeanized gentry imported into Russia from abroad.[6] This gastronomic rivalry between East and West, Visson observes, plays itself out in a number of memorable scenes from the pages of Russian fiction, from Pushkin's *Eugene Onegin* and Gogol's *Dead Souls* to Tolstoy's *Anna Karenina* and Olesha's *Envy*. In Goncharov's *Oblomov*, this gastronomic dialectic between Slavophilism and Westernism is especially apparent in the contrasting dinners that are prepared to celebrate the respective name-day feasts of Mukhoyarov and Oblomov. On St. John's Day Agafya Matveyevna's brother, who is said to be "a great epicure in affairs of gastronomy" and who "spared no expense on food" (387), invites about thirty of his colleagues to dine with him on such native fare as trout, stuffed chickens, quail, ice-cream, and wine. Ivan Matveyevich ends up spending a third of his yearly income on this one festive dinner alone. When St. Elijah's Day approaches, Oblomov seeks to outdo Agafya Matveyevna's brother by having an even more sumptuous meal prepared, one whose elegance derives primarily from the foreign, imported nature of most of the entrees:

> Oblomov not only was determined not to be outshone by Ivan Matveyevich, but did his best to impress his guests by the delicacy and elegance of the dishes unknown in that part of town. Instead of a rich kulebyaka pie there were pies so light they seemed filled with air; oysters were served before soup; there were chickens en papillote stuffed with truffles, sweetbreads, very delicate greens, and English soup. In the middle of the table there was an enormous pineapple, surrounded by peaches, apricots, and cherries. (398)

At his name-day party Oblomov thus entertains his guests with mainly "Westernized," imported food items such as oysters, truffles, and pineapple.[7]

Westernized food also figures prominently in Oblomov's dream vision of future happiness at Oblomovka. When, in part 2, Oblomov shares with Stolz his picture of the ideal life he will lead after the reorganization of his estate is completed, that picture includes such exotic culinary items as pineapple and mocha coffee, as well as such foreign imports as Havanna cigars and a hothouse. In response to Stolz's remark that his friend is describing the same sort of provincial life that their fathers and grandfathers had led, Oblomov objects strenuously: "No, I'm not. How can you say it's the same thing? Would my wife be making jams or pickling mushrooms?" (185).

"And I should not be reading last year's newspapers, travelling in an unwieldy old carriage, or eating noodle soup and roast goose," he adds, "but I should have trained my chef in the English Club or at a foreign embassy" (185). By the final part of the novel, of course, Oblomov comes to realize that the ideal of peace and repose he attains at Agafya Matveyevna's home is "shorn of poetry and bereft of the brilliance with which his imagination had once endowed the plentiful and carefree life of a country squire on his own estate, among his peasants and house-serfs" (486–87). In gastronomic terms Oblomov's dream vision of his future life may be said to have been "de-Westernized" by the excision from it of the more elegant and sophisticated aspects of European cuisine.[8] The hero himself acknowledges that the ideal he has attained in Vyborg is but a transposed and debased version of his childhood world:

> He looked upon his present way of life as a continuation of the same Oblomov-like existence, except that he lived in a different place, and the times, too, were to a certain extent different. Here, too, as at Oblomovka, he managed to strike a good bargain with life, having obtained from it a guarantee of undisturbed peace. (487)

At Agafya Matveyevna's Oblomov has also managed to obtain the guarantee of a heavy diet of Slavophilic foods that will lead to his eventual demise. Goncharov's narrator had noted early in the novel that the hero's "daily overindulgence at a meal was a kind of slow suicide" (63) and, as mentioned above, Oblomov's own doctor had warned him that if he continued eating "heavy, fatty food" (87) he would die of a stroke. And, indeed, it is largely what Visson calls an "orgy of Russian food" – hams, cheeses, dried mushrooms, sour cream, and so on – that hastens Oblomov to his premature death.[9]

For critics such as Dobrolyubov, who understand the hero's "Oblomovitis" mainly in progressive, enlightenment terms, the use of food imagery in *Oblomov* is largely satirical, since the author's presumed intention is clearly to condemn his hero's chronic lethargy and indolence as the legacy of the traditional way of provincial life for members of Russia's privileged class. According to Visson, Russian food plays a largely negative role in Oblomov, where "the overfed, pudgy child Il'ia Il'ich turns into a corpulent, slothful adult."[10] It seems to be Stolz's role periodically to remind the hero of the deleterious effect that constant overeating is having on him. "First of all you must get rid of your fat, of your bodily heaviness," he advises Oblomov in part 2 in his attempt to reform his lazy friend, "then your spirit won't be sleepy, either. You need both physical and mental gymnastics" (176). As one of the seven deadly sins, gluttony (or overeating) has long served as a target of satire for literary artists who wish to draw a contrast between the physical and spiritual or intellectual aspects of a person. The enjoyment of food and drink by fictional characters is often used to condemn the banality of those philistines who care more for stuffing their bellies than for developing their minds or elevating their souls. The actual physical consumption of food is thus frequently meant to imply a fictional character's lack of intellectual and spiritual ingestion.[11] Gogol, of course, was a master at unmasking a world of human beings devoid of an inner life by using food as a symbol of banality (*poshlost'*) and portraying people in what one critic calls "the physiology of their being."[12] Sobakievich's gluttonous gorging at the dinner table in *Dead Souls* (1842), for example, implicitly suggests his mental, moral, and emotional malnourishment. Chekhov, at century's end, would continue this Gogolian tradition of making a character's enjoyment of food and drink serve as an indicator of his essential vulgarity.[13]

In Goncharov's novel both Andrey Stolz and Olga Ilyinskaya,

neither of whom is shown very often seated at table, advance the Westernized values of intellectual, rather than merely physical, ingestion. Reading and learning represent for the two of them "the perpetual nourishment (*pitanie*) of thought and its endless development" (466). Even in childhood Stolz's home is presented as a site of Western-style (German) upbringing and education rather than of mere "feeding" – that is, of *vospitanie* in more than the narrow, literal, corporeal sense that the inhabitants of Oblomovka seem to understand the meaning of the term. "Did they know there how to rear a child?" the narrator asks rhetorically when describing life at Oblomovka. "Why you had only to look at what rosy and well-fed darlings the mothers there carried or led by the hand! It was their ambition that their children should be plump, white-skinned, and healthy" (127). The inhabitants of Oblomovka, he tells us, "took great care that the child should always be happy and eat a lot" (128). Oblomov's mother, who exacerbates her son's separation anxiety when, as a boy of thirteen or fourteen, he is sent off to school at Stolz's, is especially guilty of reducing *vospitanie* to its literal meaning. On Monday mornings, as young Oblomov prepares to set off for his lessons at Stolz's, his mother would see to it that he is sufficiently fattened up for the week:

Nothing was good enough for him to eat that morning. They baked rolls and pretzel-shaped sweet buns for him, loaded him with pickles, biscuits, jams, various fruit confections, all kinds of delicacies, both dried and in syrup, and even provisions. He was given it all on the supposition that he did not get enough to eat at the German's house: "You won't get fat there," they said at Oblomovka. "For dinner they'll give you nothing but soup, roast meat, and potatoes, and bread and butter for tea. As for supper – not a crumb, old man!" (142)[14]

Indeed, Oblomov's mother is constantly looking for an excuse to avoid sending her beloved little boy off to school. "Today is commemoration week," she observes at one point, "it's no time for lessons: we shall be baking pancakes" (142). She is instrumental in having the boy stop attending lessons at Stolz's around Easter one year, allowing him to spend the rest of spring and all of summer at home with her. "Oblomov spent a most enjoyable six months," we are told. "How tall he grew during that time! And how fat he grew! How soundly he slept!" (143). "He'll have plenty of time to study," Mrs. Oblomov reasons. "The poor boy comes back from school as from a hospital: all his fat is gone, he looks so thin" (143).

If, as some critics have argued, Oblomov later in life seeks and finds his mother once again in the person of Agafya Matveyevna, it should not surprise us that she, too, shows little interest in book learning, concerning herself exclusively with the bodily and material well-being of her gentleman boarder. When, soon after moving in, Oblomov asks his new landlady whether she reads anything, she simply stares at him with a dull, vacant expression on her face and says nothing (324). Characterized by her brother as little more than a "cow" (375), Agafya Matveyevna functions primarily as Oblomov's caretaker, providing him with ample amounts of food and drink. Indeed, the romance plot in this novel could itself be said to be structured largely on this theme of physical versus intellectual nourishment. The maidenly Olga Ilyinskaya, with her ethereal "Casta Diva" from Bellini's opera *Norma*, and the matronly Agafya Matveyevna, with her heavy meat pies, compete against each other in their efforts to provide the hero with radically differing types of sustenance: here the emotional, the cultural, and the spiritual vie directly against the physical, the domestic, and the culinary. "If the language of love in Oblomov's relationship with Olga had been flowers," Peace aptly observes, "in his relationship with Agafya Matveyevna it is quite clearly food."[15] Or, as another critic puts it, "Music, light, and lilac are pitted against casseroles, elbows, and a homely geranium plant."[16] Oblomov himself seems to recognize this competition, as he indicates in a conversation with Stolz in part 4, when he boasts about Agafya Matveyevna's ability to brew delicious homemade currant vodka. "Olga Sergeyevna won't make you any vodka like this," he brags. "She can sing 'Casta Diva' but she doesn't know how to make such vodka! Nor how to make a chicken-and-mushroom pie! Such pies they used to make only in Oblomovka and now here!" (449). In Visson's reading of the novel, as we noted earlier, Agafya Matveyevna's Slavophilic cooking signals synedochally for the reader Oblomov's backward slide into his former corpulence, sloth, and inertia; this decline culminates ultimately in a stroke caused in large part by the hero's overindulgence in food and drink.

Despite this decidedly negative role that food imagery has been seen to play in *Oblomov* as a symbol of gluttony, *poshlost'*, and intellectual as well as spiritual malnourishment, there are also some highly positive aspects to the frequent and lengthy descriptions of food preparation and scenes of eating provided in Goncharov's novel. Perhaps the most obvious one is the Homeric evocation of the earth's munificence that is conveyed through the abundance of food and drink made available to the hero first in the family kitchen at Oblomovka and then later in Agafya Matveyevna's Vyborg household. Indeed, the hero's fond reminiscences about his childhood at Oblomovka constitute the dream vision of an idyll, the type of chronotope where, as Bakhtin observes, "the association of food and children is characteristic."[17] Despite its occasionally ironic tone, "Oblomov's Dream" resonates with a kind of gastronomic lyricism, painting for the reader an enticing picture of a Russian version of the legendary Land of Cockaigne, that mythical land of abundance where food literally begs to be eaten. "Food was the first and foremost vital concern at Oblomovka," the narrator intones as he begins to describe the hero's fondest memories of his childhood years:

What calves were fattened there every year for the holidays! What birds were reared there! What deep understanding, what hard work, what care were needed in looking after them! Turkeys and chickens for name-days and other solemn occasions were fattened on nuts. Geese were deprived of exercise and hung up motionless in a sack a few days before a holiday so that they should get bloated with fat. What stores of jams, pickles, and pastries! What meads, what kvasses, were brewed, what pies baked at Oblomovka! (115)

Drawn to daydreaming about the security, warmth, and comfort of his childhood spent in rural Oblomovka as a way to escape the harsh realities of his adult life in bustling St. Petersburg, Oblomov returns in his imagination to this gastronomic "paradise lost" whose images, as Ehre notes, are presented in "homely and domestic terms" that center on the preparation and consumption of food.[18] The idyllic vision of Ilya Ilyich's childhood makes his birthplace quite literally into an Arcadian "land of milk and honey" that provides him not only full satisfaction of his oral appetites but also the emotional nourishment he craves. "The enumeration of the gustatory delights of this Russian land of Cockayne is like an incantation to security," Milton Mays observes. "Little Oblomov enjoys a regime much like that of the Oblomovka geese, marinated in affection as in goodies."[19]

With his imagination enflamed by his nanny's fairy tales about some wonderful country "where rivers flowed with milk and honey, where no one did a stroke of work all year round" (120), the adult Oblomov seeks to find a real-life version of Militrissa Kirbityevna, the legendary maiden of indescribable beauty who inhabits this magical kingdom and who personifies the plenitude and solicitude that reign there. And he seems eventually to find her – not, however, in the beautiful music and delicate flowers of the vivacious Olga Ilyinskaya, but rather in the delicious soups and homemade pies of the hospitable Agafya Matveyevna, whose gastronomically significant surname Pshenitsyna (wheat), one critic observes, "implies both sustenance and fecundity."[20] What the hero had been searching for all along was not actually a wife but rather a mother: not a young and vital life partner who will make it necessary for him to exhibit adult responsibility as well as mature (genital) sexuality, but a matronly cook who, in addition to nurturing and protecting this overgrown child, will satisfy his oral needs by providing him with tasty meals. After all, the only eroticism the infantile Oblomov seems interested in, one critic notes, is a "gustatory" one.[21] "He looked at her," the narrator writes of Oblomov and Agafya Matveyevna, "with the same pleasure with which he looked at her hot curd-cheese tarts that morning" (347). Oblomov, we are told, sees in Agafya Matveyevna with her perpetually moving elbows, her watchful, solicitous eyes, her perpetual trips from the cupboard to the kitchen, from the kitchen to the pantry, and from there to the cellar, her thorough knowledge of housekeeping and all domestic comforts, the embodied ideal of that life of boundless – like an ocean – and inviolate repose, the picture of which had been ineradicably imprinted on his soul in childhood, under his father's roof. As in Oblomovka his father, his grandfather, the children, the grandchildren, and the visitors sat or lay about in idle repose, knowing that there were in the house unsleeping eyes that watched over them continually and never-weary hands that sewed their clothes, gave them food and drink, clothed and shod them, put them to bed, and closed their eyes when they were dead, so here, too, Oblomov, sitting on the sofa from which he never stirred, saw that something nimble and lively was moving for his benefit, and that if the sun should not rise tomorrow, whirlwinds cloud the sky, a stormy wind blow from one end of the earth to the other, his soup and roast would be on his table. (394)

At Agafya Matveyevna's apartment the hero thus realizes the Oblomovkan ideal of childhood that he had sought in vain in his relationship with Olga Ilyinskaya, whose vitality and sexual passion had scared him off, threatening to shatter his idyllic dream. "Failing to find the idyll in one woman, Oblomov recovers it in the other," Ehre explains. "The novel has described a complete circle, from dream to dream, from idyll to idyll, from the momentary vision of a lost paradise to its momentary realization."[22]

Understood in this way, as a movement from "paradise lost" to "paradise regained,"[23] Oblomov's quest to return to the idyllic condition of his Oblomovkan childhood involves a psychological regression to a carefree, presexual existence where libidinal pleasure is derived primarily, if not exclusively, from the ingestion of food and drink. Oblomov's return to this childhood paradise is signaled gastronomically by the reappearance in parts 3 and 4 of the enticing smell of delicious chicken-and-mushroom pies and of the familiar sound of the clatter of knives chopping meat and vegetables that emanate from his landlady's kitchen.[24] In food terms, the reader becomes aware that Oblomov in Vyborg has regained his lost paradise by noting the resemblance that the cooking and housekeeping at Agafya Matveyevna's bears to the hero's idyllic memories of home life at Oblomovka. Walking into the courtyard of Agafya Matveyevna's home, one finds oneself in the midst of what the narrator calls a "living idyll" (482), an impression that continues once inside the house as well:

> Everything in Pshenitsyna's home breathed such household abundance and plenitude. . . . The kitchen, the pantries, the sideboard were all supplied with cabinets filled with crockery, dishes large and small, round and oval, sauce-boats, cups, piles of plates, and iron, copper, and earthenware pots. . . . There were huge glass jars of coffee, cinnamon, and vanilla, crystal tea-caddies, cruets of oil and vinegar. Then whole shelves were loaded with packets, vials, boxes of household remedies, herbs, lotions, plasters, spirits, camphor, simple and fumigatory powders; there was also soap, material for cleaning lace, taking out stains, and so on, and so on – everything that a good housekeeper in the provinces keeps in her house. . . . In the larder smoked hams were suspended from the ceiling, so that mice could not get at them, as well as cheeses, sugar-loaves, cured fish, bags of dried mushrooms, and nuts bought from Finnish peddlers. On the floor stood tubs of butter, huge, covered earthenware jugs of sour cream, baskets of eggs, and lots of other things! (482–83)

"One would need the pen of another Homer," the narrator adds, "to describe fully and in detail all that had been accumulated in all the corners and on all the shelves of this small ark of domestic life" (483). Agafya Matveyevna's well-stocked larder, as an embodiment of plenty, thus promises Oblomov the appeasement of his physical and emotional hunger through unbounded motherly love.[25]

The historical and cultural analogue to Oblomov's regression wish is the hero's desire to return to an earlier, prelapsarian stage in

Russia's historical development: to return, that is, to an idyllic Golden Age of patriarchal relations that is imagined as having existed before the advent of modernization, which disrupted autochthonous culture, and its primitive natural economy, through industrialization, secularization, and urbanization.[26] Understood in this historical and national context, Oblomov is experiencing nostalgia for a more primitive but happier way of life that is believed to have existed in his nation's past; he is longing to return to a mythic Slavic Ausonia, where communalism and commensalism – rather than individualism and differentiation – shaped human relationships. The literary genre of neopastoral that arose in the wake of the industrial revolution, Raymond Williams has observed, invariably portrayed an idyllic life characterized by what he calls the "happy ethic of consuming," where the dining table – as the site of hospitable eating and drinking – plays a central role in conveying a spirit of community.[27] As Michel Jeanneret observes in his study of Renaissance banqueting, "at table we rediscover, in the imagination, elements of original happiness and unity."[28] The Oblomovka meals that Oblomov reminisces about in dream visions of his childhood past convey a precapitalist kinship model and a connection with folk mythology that have at their center a sense of nurturing, harmony, and communion, all of which the hero, as an adult, finds woefully lacking in the bustling St. Petersburg life that surrounds him. Whereas in Oblomovka a ritualistic attitude toward the renewal of life that comes each year at springtime is manifested by the traditional baking of "larks," it is "the importing of oysters and lobsters which defines Spring for the inhabitants of St. Petersburg."[29] Likewise, in Oblomovka, the ritual preparation of dinner is seen largely as a communal activity: "The whole household was consulted about the dinner: the aged aunt, too, was invited to the council. Each person suggested his or her own dish: one person giblet soup, another noodle soup or brawn, another tripe, another red or white sauce. Every advice was taken into consideration, thoroughly discussed, and then accepted or rejected in accordance with the final decision of the mistress of the house" (114–15). In cosmopolitan St. Petersburg, on the other hand, meals are prepared and served more privately and individually, without any of this communitarian spirit.

Not only are the plans and preparations for a meal done collectively in Oblomovka, so too is its consumption: remnants of the large stuffed pie, baked for the master on Sundays and holidays, would be eaten throughout the rest of the week by members of the family as well as by the maids and house serfs. Iury Loshchits, who refers to Goncharov's style in the novel as a kind of "mythological realism,"[30] notes that the communal eating of this enormous pie, a food item meant to symbolize prosperity and well-being, apotheosizes not only the feeling of satiety enjoyed by the inhabitants of Oblomovka but also their folkloric sense of belonging to a greater and more meaningful whole:

> What, after all, is Oblomov's existence, if not the fragment of a life that at one time was full-valued and all-embracing? And what is Oblomovka, if not a "blessed corner" forgotten by everyone and remaining intact due to a miracle – a fragment of Eden? The local inhabitants eat up an archeological fragment, a piece of what was once an enormous pie. We recall that in the folk *Weltanschaung* the pie is one of the most graphic symbols of a happy, abundant, prosperous life. The pie is a "lavish feast," a cornucopia, the acme of universal merriment and contentment. Around the pie gathers the feasting, festive folk. From the pie emanates warmth and fragrance; the pie is the central and most archaic symbol of the folk utopia. It is not for nothing that a very real cult of the pie reigns in Oblomovka. The preparation of an enormous pastry and its consumption recall a kind of sacramental ceremony which is strictly fulfilled according to the calendar, from week to week, and month to month. The "dream kingdom" of Oblomovka revolves around its pie, as if around a hot, luminous sphere.[31]

The "(w)holistic" nature of this imagined community at Oblomovka, a community that seems free of any sense of disharmony, exclusion, or class conflict, is especially visible at the dinner table. "Food and drink in the idyll partake of a nature that is social or, more often, family," Bakhtin reminds us, "all *generations* and *age-groups* come together around the table."[32] Thus young Oblomov's typical day, at age seven, would begin with him being caressed lovingly by family and friends gathered around the breakfast table, adults who offer him their affection and acceptance by way of kisses, hugs, and food. "All these members of the Oblomov retinue and establishment picked up the little boy and began showering him with caresses and praises," the narrator relates, "he had hardly time to wipe away the traces of the unbidden kisses. After that they began stuffing him with rolls, biscuits, and cream. Then his mother hugged and kissed him again" (111).

This warm, loving atmosphere of Oblomovkan commensality is markedly absent, of course, from the rather lonely bachelor life that Oblomov leads as an adult in the capital, where – as a "spiritual exile"[33] – he is usually shown to be dining alone at home. "Waking up, he saw the table set for dinner: cold fish soup with beet greens and kvass, and tenderized cutlet," we read in part 2. "He had his dinner and sat down by the window. It was so boring, so absurd – always alone!" (235). Even when he does dine out with others rather than eat alone at home, Oblomov continues to pine for the spirit of communion and commensality that he remembers and idealizes from his childhood. What he particularly dislikes about the bustling St. Petersburg lifestyle to which Stolz is seeking to reintroduce him during part 2 of the novel is precisely this conspicuous lack of love, fellowship, and goodwill at table. The members of this urbane society, he complains, young and old alike,

> gather, entertain each other at meals, but there is no real good-fellowship, no real hospitality, no mutual attraction. If they gather at a dinner or a party, it is just the same as at their office – coldly, without a spark of gaiety, to boast of their chef or their drawing room, and then to jeer at each other in a discreet aside, to trip one another up. The other day at dinner I honestly did not know where to look and wished I could hide under the table, when they began tearing to shreds the reputations of those who did not

happen to be there: "This one is a fool, that one is a mean scoundrel; another one is a thief; and another one is ridiculous" – a regular massacre! . . . Why, then, do they come together if they are like that? Why do they press each other's hands so warmly? No genuine laughter, not a glimmer of sympathy! (180)

It is worth noting that Oblomov, whose early retirement from government service stemmed largely from the disenchantment and disappointment he felt when he realized that the civil servants employed in one department were not "one big happy family, unremittingly concerned about one another's peace and pleasures" (58), experiences terrible embarrassment and discomfort when he dines for the first time with Olga Ilyinskaya. "The footman brought him a cup of tea and a tray with cakes," the narrator relates. "He wanted to suppress his feeling of embarrassment and to be free and easy – and picked up such a pile of rusks, biscuits and cakes that a little girl who sat next to him giggled. Others eyed the pile curiously" (197). The hero suffers "the same agonies at dinner" (200) on the following day, when once again he finds himself struggling to remain calm and relaxed under Olga's watchful gaze at the dinner table. "It's sheer agony!" he laments. "Have I come here to be laughed at by her?" (200).

Later, in part 2, Oblomov's earlier embarrassment at Olga noticing his *gaucherie* with the biscuits returns in the form of the severe self-consciousness he suffers at her aunt's dinner table, where, at the mere mention of a love story, he "would suddenly seize, in his confusion, such a fistful of rusks that someone was quite sure to laugh" (277). By part 3 of the novel Oblomov's embarrassment, discomfort, and self-consciousness at the dinner table turns into deep anxiety as the panic-stricken suitor imagines how his health will be toasted at the official dinner specially given to celebrate his engagement to Olga (351). Being betrothed to Olga, in Oblomov's view, would mean that "you must never eat and drink properly and adequately, but live on air and bouquets!" (332).[34] When, in his attempt to flee from the harsh psychological and emotional realities he encounters in St. Petersburg, Oblomov imagines what his ideal future life in the country will be like; that rural idyll is replete not only with abundant meals and tasty foods but also with the companionship of a kind helpmate and a warm atmosphere of fellowship and goodwill among family and friends. "You will not hear someone delivering a violent philippic against an absent friend," Oblomov tells Stolz when he describes how a meal will be enjoyed in this future life. "You will not catch a glance that promises the same to you the moment you leave the house. You will not break bread with anyone you do not like. You will see sympathy in the eyes of your companions, sincere and good-natured laughter in their jokes. . . . Everything is to one's liking! Everybody looks and says what is in his heart!" (185). Happiness for Oblomov thus consists not merely in having copious amounts of delicious food to eat and beverages to drink but also in sharing the dining experience with people whom he loves and who love him: his ideal meal is characterized by a relaxing spirit of communion, fellowship, and goodwill that envelopes everyone there at table.

Oblomov seems eventually to regain this commensal spirit that he remembers from his Oblomovka childhood and that he projects into the ideal future life he fantasizes about. He recaptures it around the family dinner table at Agafya Matveyevna's home, where his meals are now taken in the pleasant company of the landlady herself, her young children, and, on occasion, his friend Alexeyev. One of the hero's favorite activities in his Vyborg life consists in loading his family into a carriage and driving out to the Gunpowder Works for a picnic on his name-day (488). Indeed, Oblomov wishes to share the happiness of these family excursions with his old friend Stolz and his wife Olga, suggesting they purchase a summer cottage nearby so that the couple could join him and his new family in such pleasant activities. "You'd love it!" he gushes to Stolz. "We'd have tea in the woods, go to the Gunpowder Works on St. Elijah's Day, with a cart laden with provisions and samovar following us. We'd lie down on the grass there – on a rug! Agafya Matveyevna would teach Olga Sergeyevna how to run a house. Truly she would!" (449). In his daydreams about an ideal future life, picnicking with family and friends on the grass and sharing food as well as fellowship likewise constitute an instantiation of the Oblomovkan spirit of commensality that Oblomov desperately seeks to recapture in his adult life. He comes closest to attaining it at Agafya Matveyevna's home, where "everything of a hostile nature had disappeared from Oblomov's life" (485). "He was now surrounded by simple, kind, and loving people," the narrator informs us, "who all consented to do their best to make his life as comfortable as possible" (485).

Psychoanalytical readings of *Oblomov*, John Givens points out in his insightful essay in this volume, often interpret this novel as the story of the hero's desire to return to the womb.[35] Leon Stilman, for example, argues that Oblomov's regression wish betrays his desire to return to the peace, calm, and repose of the prenatal state.[36] Although it is possible to find evidence in Goncharov's novel to support such an interpretation, the food imagery in *Oblomov*, it seems to me, suggests that the hero's regression wish is not so much a death wish as a longing to recapture what Natalie Baratoff, in her Jungian analysis of the novel, calls "the original maternal symbiosis": that is, the perfect symbiotic union of the pre-Oedipal child feeding at the mother's breast.[37] In Goncharov's novel food is made to serve, among other things, as an emblem of all the comfort, security, and warmth that characterize the hero's idealized infantile past; it represents a lost state of total unity and undifferentiated oneness with the mother that exists in very early childhood, during the oral stage, before the infant is weaned away from the maternal breast.[38] Hence the magnetic appeal that Oblomov finds in the high, firm bosom of Agafya Matveyevna, who becomes at once his surrogate mother and nanny substitute.[39] If, as some critics have suggested, Agafya Matveyevna is depicted as a Christian image of the Virgin Mother, then her iconic representation is probably best captured in medieval paintings of the "suckling" Madonna, who is portrayed as nursing the infant Jesus at her breast.[40] As Givens explains,

Agafya Matveyevna becomes for Oblomov and the reader that part of the mother's anatomy from which nourishment and sensual pleasure is first derived, the place between the crook of the elbows cradling the child and holding it to the exposed breast which feeds it and the bare arms and shoulders which form the borders of the baby's world during feeding.[41]

Through his regression wish, the hero may ultimately be seeking a return to the dark stillness of the mother's womb, but the numerous gastronomic motifs in *Oblomov* seem to indicate that the main object of his regressive desire may well be the maternal breast that nourishes the suckling infant. In psychoanalytical terms, Oblomov – like many of Gogol's adult male characters who seem to "retreat" from the demands of romantic love – may be said to be regressing from mature adult genitality to oral modes of libidinal expression, which are manifested in his extreme fondness for eating and drinking.[42]

The general ailment that afflicts humankind, Oblomov might argue, is not so much the "curse of being born."[43] Rather, it is the necessity of being weaned from the maternal breast and thus being forced to abandon the symbiosis that is enjoyed during infancy, when the pre-Oedipal child is fed, caressed, and protected within an atmosphere of unconditional love and affection. Weaning, not birth, would seem to constitute the true "fall" of humankind, for it signals the end of the spirit of communion that characterizes the original maternal symbiosis. The childhood paradise Oblomov envisions (and seeks to regain) is not only blessed by a plenitude of food that symbolizes the earth's munificence but is also characterized by a state of love, harmony, and bonding that is conveyed in large part by commensality at table. Eating, Oblomov's consuming passion, serves, therefore, as the physical manifestation not merely of his passion to "consume" but also of his desire to "consummate" and "commune": of his deep-seated wish to become one with the "other" – whether that "other" be his mother, his family, his friends, or the entire world. The communal dining table, as much as the mother's protective womb or the nanny's nursing breast, functions as the destination of Oblomov's psychic quest to return home. It is there that this Russian Odysseus in bed slippers can feast once again at the banquet of a harmonious Edenic life, eating his piece of a big, round, wholesome pie in a convivial atmosphere of love, fellowship, and goodwill.[44]

NOTES

I would like to thank Joyce Toomre, Darra Goldstein, and Musya Glants for their help in translating some of the culinary terms in *Oblomov*.

1. Iury Loshchits, *Goncharov* (Moscow: Molodaia gvardiia, 1977), p. 171.

2. I. A. Goncharov, *Sobranie sochinenii v vos' mi tomakh*, vol. 4 (Moscow: Khudozhestvennaia literatura, 1953), p. 87. All further references to *Oblomov* come from this edition of Goncharov' s works and will be cited parenthetically in the text. I am using, with some slight modifications, the English translation provided by David Magarshack in Ivan Goncharov, *Oblomov* (New York: Penguin, 1967).

3. Mikhail Bakhtin, *Rabelais and His World*, trans. Helene Iswolsky (Cambridge: MIT Press, 1968), p. 281.

4. For affinities between Flemish genre paintings and pictorial representation in early nineteenth-century Russian prose, see my two articles "Teniersism: Seventeenth-Century Flemish Art and Early Nineteenth-Century Russian Prose," *The Russian Review*, 49 (1990): 19–41; and "Teniers, Flemish Art, and the Natural School Debate," *Slavic Review* 50, no. 3 (1991): 576–89. Alexander Druzhinin draws attention to the close parallels that may be said to exist between Goncharov' s prose and Flemish art in his review of *Oblomov* that appeared in *Biblioteka dlia chteniia* in 1859. See Druzhinin, *Literaturnaia kritika* (Moscow: Sovetskaia Rossiia, 1983), pp. 296–98.

5. James Brown examines the various uses of food imagery in works by these and other nineteenth-century French authors in his book *Fictional Meals and Their Function in the French Novel, 1789–1848* (Toronto: University of Toronto Press, 1984). For a gastrocritical study of Flaubert, see Lilian R. Furst, "The Role of Food in *Madame Bovary*," *Orbis Litterarium* 34, no. 1 (1979): 52–65.

6. Lynn Visson, "Kasha vs. Cachet Blanc: The Gastronomic Dialectics of Russian Literature," in *Russianness: Studies on a Nation's Identity. In Honor of Rufus Mathewson*, ed. Robert Belknap (Ann Arbor, Mich.: Ardis, 1990), pp. 60–73.

7. "French and English dishes," Visson asserts, "still represent fashion, aristocracy, and gentility for the lazy and rapidly deteriorating Oblomov" (see ibid., p. 67).

8. As Visson puts it, "the more he [Oblomov] slides into inertia, the greater the role of 'Russian' food" (see ibid).

9. Ibid., p. 68.

10. Ibid., p. 66.

11. In Russian literature this is especially true of comic writers such as Gogol, Chekhov, and Bulgakov. For the latter's treatment of the theme of gluttony, see my article "Stomaching Philistinism: Griboedov House and the Symbolism of Eating in *The Master and Margarita*," in *The Master and Margarita: A Critical Companion*, ed. Laura Weeks (Evanston, Ill.: Northwestern University Press, 1996), pp. 172–92.

12. Natalia M. Kolb-Seletski, "Gastronomy, Gogol, and His Fiction," *Slavic Review* 1 (1970): 48. For Gogol's use of food imagery, see also Alexander P. Obolensky, *Food-Notes on Gogol* (Winnipeg: Trident, 1972). Vasily Gippius refers to this physiological interest among characters in Gogol's works as "visceralness" ("fiziologichnost'"). See *Gogol*, trans. Robert A. Maguire (Durham, N.C.: Duke University Press, 1989), p. 129.

13. For an interesting treatment of this topic, see Nils Åke Nilsson, "Food Images in Cechov. A Bachtinian Approach," in *Scando-Slavica* 32 (1986): 27–40.

14. Zakhar likewise closely identifies living "like a German" with leading a niggardly material existence. "Just look at how they live! The whole family gnaws a bone all week long," he complains about Germans early in part 1. "They don't collect a whole corner full of crusts of bread during the winter. They don't waste a single crust, they don't! They make them into rusks and drink them with their beer!" (15–16).

15. Richard Peace, *Oblomov: A Critical Examination of Goncharov's Novel* (Birmingham: University of Birmingham, 1991), p. 59.

16. Milton Ehre, *Oblomov and His Creator: The Life and Art of Ivan Goncharov* (Princeton, N.J.: Princeton University Press, 1973), p. 208.

17. Bakhtin, *Rabelais*, p. 227.

18. Ehre, *Oblomov and His Creator*, p. 175.

19. Milton Mays, "Oblomov as Anti-Faust," *Western Humanities Review*, 21, no. 2 (1967): 147.

20. Darra Goldstein, "Domestic Porkbarreling in Nineteenth-Century

Russia, or Who Holds the Keys to the Larder?" in *Russia.Women.Culture*, ed. Helena Goscilo and Beth Holmgren (Bloomington: Indiana University Press, 1996), p. 132.

21. Mays, "Oblomov as Anti-Faust," p. 151.

22. Ehre, *Oblomov and His Creator*, p. 224. "Olga represented a false and illusory idyll," Ehre maintains, "the discovery of the idyll in Agafya Matveevna is the true 'working out of the motive' of the novel" (224–25).

23. Mays, "Oblomov as Anti-Faust," p. 144.

24. Commenting on the matriarchy described at Oblomovka, Alexandra and Sverre Lyngstad write: "Life centered on food, and the 'clatter of knives' in the kitchen is a dominant motif both in 'Oblomov' s Dream' and in his reveries about the ideal life; it is also prominent in the Vyborg chapters" (see their *Ivan Goncharov* (New York: Twayne, 1971), p. 90.

25. Goldstein, "Domestic Porkbarreling," p. 130.

26. I explore this issue more deeply in a conference paper, "Gastronomic Slavophilism: The Myth of the Russian Gentry Estate as a Pastoral Paradise," which was presented at the Second Interdisciplinary Conference on Food and Culture, held at Boston University in May 1995.

27. Raymond Williams, *The Country and the City* (New York: Oxford University Press, 1973), p. 30.

28. Michel Jeanneret, *A Feast of Words: Banquets and Table Talk in the Renaissance*, trans. Jeremy Whiteley and Emma Hughes (Chicago: University of Chicago Press, 1991), p. 2.

29. Peace, *Oblomov: A Critical Examination*, p. 31.

30. Loshchits, *Goncharov*, p. 169.

31. Ibid., pp. 172–73.

32. Bakhtin, *Rabelais*, p. 227. Agafya Matveyevna' s brother seems to represent the counterforce to this commensal and communal spirit at table. Early in part 4 it is pointed out that Ivan Matveyevich dined alone, eating at a later time, separately from his sister and her children, mostly in the kitchen (388).

33. Lyngstads, *Ivan Goncharov*, p. 78.

34. The reader gets the sense, from a brief humorous exchange that takes place between Oblomov and Zakhar in part 2, chapter 8, that Olga – much like Stolz – is given to teasing the hero about his rather hearty appetite. "I said, sir, that you had dinner at home, and supper at home, too," Zakhar reports back about a conversation he had with Olga. "Why, the young lady

asks, does he have supper? Well, sir, I told her you had only two chickens for supper." "Well, what did she say?" Oblomov asks nervously. "She smiled, sir. Why so little? she asked" (236–37). As Peace notes, Olga "coaxes him [Oblomov] out of eating supper (a provincial custom frowned on in St. Petersburg, as we learn from *A Common Story*)" (see p. 48).

35. See Givens's essay, "Wombs, Tombs, and Mother Love: A Freudian Reading of Goncharov's *Oblomov*," in this volume.

36. Leon Stilman, "Oblomovka Revisited," *The American Slavic and East European Review* 7 (1948): 68.

37. Natalie Baratoff, *Oblomov: A Jungian Approach. A Literary Image of the Mother Complex* (New York: Peter Lang, 1990), p. 106.

38. Maggie Kilgour, *From Communion to Cannibalism: An Anatomy of Metaphors of Incorporation* (Princeton, N.J.: Princeton University Press, 1990), p. 5.

39. "Connoting a rudimentary desire, along with the infantile need for a mother's care and an inexorable urge for a life of indolence," the Lyngstads observe, "this image [Agafya Matveyevna' s bosom] sums up Oblomov's 'dream,' 'the paradisal life'" (see their *Ivan Goncharov*, p. 90). For an interesting feminist reading that explores the political significance of images of breast-feeding in nineteenth-century Russian fiction, see Jane Costlow' s essay, "The Pastoral Source: Representations of the Maternal Breast in Nineteenth-Century Russia," in *Sexuality and the Body in Russian Culture*, ed. Jane Costlow, Stephanie Sandler, and Judith Vowles (Stanford: Stanford University Press, 1993), pp. 223–36.

40. It is Yvette Louria and Morton I. Seiden who interpret Goncharov's portrayal of Agafya Matveyevna in Christian iconic terms. See their article, "Ivan Goncharov' s *Oblomov*: The Anti-Faust as Christian Hero," in *Canadian Slavic Studies* 3, no. 1 (1969): 39–68. For a brief discussion of icons of the nursing Virgin, or "suckling Madonna"(*Madonna del Latte*), see Allen J. Grieco, *Themes in Art: The Meal* (London: Scala Publications, 1992), p. 13.

41. See Givens's article in this volume.

42. See Hugh McLean, "Gogol's Retreat from Love: Toward an Interpretation of *Mirgorod*," in *Russian Literature and Psychoanalysis*, ed. Daniel Rancour-Laferriere (Amsterdam and Philadelphia: John Benjamins, 1989), pp. 101–22.

43. See Givens's article in this volume.

44. In Book 9, chapter 5 of *Tom Jones* (1749), Henry Fielding pays tribute

to the hearty appetite of Homer's epic hero. Fielding apologizes, in mock heroic style, for the "good stomach" of his young hero, Tom Jones, noting that "it may be doubted whether *Ulysses*, who by the Way seems to have had the best Stomach of all the Heroes in that eating poem of the *Odyssey*, ever made a better Meal" (see Fielding, *Tom Jones*, ed. Sheridan Baker [New York: W. W. Norton, 1973], p. 387).

III  PRIMARY SOURCES

Correspondence Relating to *Oblomov*

Translated from the Russian by

BRIAN THOMAS OLES

TO A. A. KRAEVSKY[1]

Simbirsk, 25 September 1849

My dear Andrey Aleksandrovich,

You have probably been thinking until now that I had disappeared without a trace, so I am sending you my latest *news* – but, unfortunately, no *novel* ["shliu . . . *vest'*, a ne *povest* ' "]. I am aware that I have a lot to answer for, and furthermore that the excuses I can offer in my own defense will probably seem inadequate to anyone except myself. Who needs to know that I cannot just dash something off when I happen to have a day or hour free, that *things get worked out in my head slowly and painfully*, finally that, *as the years go by, I am struck less and less with the desire to write* – and that without this I will never write anything? I came here thinking that the quiet and free time would allow me to continue the work I had begun, and with which you are already familiar [i. e., *Oblomov*]. That might have been the case, had the work itself allowed me to continue it. On carefully rereading what was already written, however, I realized that it was all trite [*poshlo*] in the extreme, that I had taken the wrong approach to my subject, that one thing needed to be edited, another omitted entirely – in short, that my work was practically worthless. . . .

So this is the sad state I now find myself in. I would have written you about it a long time ago, but I continued to hope that I would manage to get something done. I locked myself in my room every morning to work, but despite painful effort everything would turn out wordy and unpolished, like so much raw material. The days kept passing, and now suddenly I am leaving for Petersburg the day after tomorrow with nothing but a dubious hope for future productivity – dubious because in Petersburg once again I won't be free during the mornings, and, finally, because I fear that with age I may have actually lost the ability to write.

Anyway, in order assuage my guilt a little, I am prepared if you wish to surrender the beginning of my novel – as bad as it is – by the first of the year. In this case, however, I would work on it no further, since any continuation would demand a new beginning, as well. . . .

TO E. V. TOLSTAYA[2]

Petersburg, 31 December 1855

. . . You ask about my novel – ah, you're not the only one! My editors are even worse than you with their questions, and there are three of them at once, so that even if I were to finish it and manage to satisfy one, I still don't know how I would be rid of the other two.[3] Anyway, there is still no sign of a novel. An expedition report, a travel log, yes – but not a novel: this demands auspicious, even fortuitous, conditions. The imagination, whose involvement is as essential to writing a novel as it is to a poem, is like a flower that blooms sweetly in the sun's rays – it needs the rays of . . . *good fortune* to blossom. But where can I find them? Mine have faded, old age is covering my eyes like a hat pulled down too far. Melancholy has been gnawing at me to the point of physical illness – and meanwhile I am bound for hectic, intense work. How to get out of it I don't know – I'd like to run away from both responsibilities and people, but I can't. The matter of my position [i. e., as a censor] should be decided next month – there will probably be a vacancy . . .

TO I. I. LKHOVSKY[4]

Marienbad, 15 July, 1857

. . . You should know I'm caught up in something – and, yes, you wouldn't be mistaken if you guessed it was a woman. Never mind that I'm forty-five, still I'm utterly taken with Olga Ilyinskaya (only not the countess, a different one). No sooner have I drunk my three glasses of water and run all over Marienbad from six to nine in the morning having barely managed to grab some tea, as I take my cigar and go to her. Then I sit in her room, go to the park, steal through some secluded lane and can't for the life of me get enough of her. I do have a rival who, though younger than I, is also more awkward – I hope to drive them apart soon. Then I'll leave with her for Frankfurt, and then on to Switzerland or perhaps straight to Paris, I don't know yet. Everything depends on whether or not I win her over. If I do, we'll return to Petersburg together and then you will see her and decide for yourself whether she merits the passionate attentions I've been paying her, or is nothing special – a dull, pallid woman who shines in my loving eyes only. If you think that, then perhaps I'll become disillusioned and abandon her. But for now . . . for now my excitement verges on madness: even when I was young it was never like this. I can hardly sit still, I pace the floor rapidly, my mind working overtime. I feel I could even write something, if only my doctors hadn't forbidden it. Stimulation is hazardous to my health, and I'm certainly stimulated. . . . I know you're shaking your head and having a good laugh at my expense; maybe you're even pitying me. Don't pity me: I'm happy from nine to three every day – who could ask for more? This woman, of course, is my own written creation. Well? Are you so obtuse that you still haven't guessed I've been writing?

TO IU. D. EFREMOVA[5]

Marienbad, 29 July 1857

. . . Well then, listen to this: I arrived here on June 21 by the Russian calendar. Now it's July 29 and I have *finished the first and second parts of Oblomov, and have written a good bit of the third* – so I can see the end in the distance through the trees. It must seem strange – even impossible – that almost a whole novel could be written in a month. But you must remember that, in the first place, it had been ripening in my mind for many years – practically all that was left for me to do was write it down; second, it's not done yet; third, it will require considerable editing; and, finally, fourth, perhaps I have written a heap of rubbish good only for immolation. Then again, perhaps – God willing – it will be good for something besides that, so I won't throw it into the fire yet. I would gladly stay here another month, because I know that after I leave I will no longer be able to devote myself exclusively to writing. However, I am not staying because, even despite my other work, it won't be difficult to complete the unfinished portion of the novel in Petersburg. The main thing, the part that called for peaceful solitude and excitement – to wit, the woman whom it was my main goal to depict, the heart and soul of the novel – is written; Oblomov's love story is finished. Whether it is good or bad is not for me to decide. . . . For my part, I did the best I could. Now that this is all over, though, I will never write anything again. And don't you dare say that I will – shame on you! I'm worn out enough as it is.

TO I. I. LKHOVSKY

Marienbad, 2 August 1857

. . . Yes, Horatio my son – there are some things our press correspondents have never dreamed of. Just imagine, if you can: I arrived here on June 21 (Russian calendar), and within three days was so bored I wanted to leave. For three or four days I wrote letters – to you, to Iazykov, to Simbirsk – for want of something else to do. Then around the twenty-fifth or twenty-sixth I inadvertently opened *Oblomov* and caught fire: by the thirty-first this hand had written forty-seven pages! *I have edited and finished the first part, written the second, and made quite a dent in the third.* Frankel, my doctor, saw how bored I was at first and how I subsequently relaxed when I began to work – initially, he was pleased to find me writing at my desk. But on finding me there at ten, then at one, then at three o'clock, he started complaining and trying to calm me down. Now he is running around telling all the Russian patients that I will never be cured because I am always busy with my *statistics!* . . . Frankel also gave me his books on Marienbad; he thinks I am writing a description of the place – and of him – for a Russian audience. Let him think that! . . .

I do not know if I have recovered fully, only that I have around three weeks of intense work left before I finish *Oblomov*. I've had my nose to the grindstone a long time already. The courtly love poem is all done – it took up a lot of time and space. It must seem odd: how could someone suddenly finish in one month something he was unable to finish for years? To this I respond that if it hadn't been for those years nothing would have been written in that month. The fact is that the novel, down to its smallest scenes and details, burst forth all at once – all that was left was to write it down. I wrote as though taking dictation. Really – a lot of it simply appeared, unconsciously: someone invisible sat next to me and told me what to write. For example, in my plan for the novel I had envisioned a *passionate* woman, but my pencil completely altered this central attribute and filled in the rest accordingly. Thus a different figure emerged. . . . I worry sometimes that I don't have a single real-life *type* in the novel, only ideal people. Is that all right? At the same time, I do not need real types to express my main idea – indeed they would deflect me from my purpose. Or rather I need a huge talent like Gogol's to rein in both the real and the ideal. My fears that my style is too simple, that I cannot write à la Turgenev, subsided when the whole picture of *Oblomov* began to come into focus: I realized that the point isn't my style but the integrity of the whole construction. It was as though a large city came into my view; the reader is placed where he can observe this city in its entirety, and he looks for its edges and center, tries to see how its outskirts relate to the city as a whole, where its towers and parks are located – but does not bother with whether the buildings are of stone or brick, whether the roofing material is smooth, what shape the windows are, etc., etc. This grand fairy tale should make an impression, I think, but what kind and how deep – I cannot yet tell. Perhaps the protagonist is incomplete – one or another side of him not sufficiently developed, a good deal left unsaid – but I am already comfortable even with this. What is the reader for, anyway? Is he really such a moron that he cannot fill in the rest based on the author's main idea? . . . The author's task is to suggest the character's prevailing disposition; the rest is up to the reader. . . .

I am not flapping my wings about like some rooster, though, crowing about my brilliant success when I do not know on what dunghill I will land. So please tell Iuninka [Efremova], whom I wrote about the novel, not to make too much noise about it. What's the use? I'll probably be so ashamed of it that I'll have to keep it under wraps. Take, for example, the woman Oblomov is in love with, Olga Sergeyevna Ilyinskaya: she may be such a hideous outcome of a listless, spent imagination that she ought to be changed completely or gotten rid of altogether. I don't know myself what to do with her. At first she seemed an icon of simplicity and virtue – but later, it would appear, that image ruptured and disintegrated. I don't know – perhaps this is all very silly. I am at a loss; sometimes I just want to leave right away for Lausanne, or Bern, or Vevey, lock myself up for another month there, then return and tell everyone, "I've finished, understand? Finished!" I can already hear your diffident words, can imagine you treating me to delicious, tender praise one teaspoon at a time, Turgenev's bear hugs, and the tacit, suppressed irritation of those people who hate to see others succeed. But I view this happy scene as a dream unlikely to come true. . . . And it is terrifying to think how much is left to edit; the only comfort is that editing is not real work but pleasure. How on earth did this happen? How did I – an exhausted, hardened man indifferent to everything, even his own success – suddenly resume a project I had given up on? If only you had seen how I was working! I could hardly contain my excitement: my head was pounding, Louisa [his maid] would find me in tears, I would pace the floor like a madman, couldn't feel my legs under me as I ran through the hills and woods. Even when I was young, nothing like this ever happened to me. Alas, however, there is a simple explanation. Marienbad water is terrifically stimulating; this is why they give it to people suffering from high blood pressure only with great discretion and in very small amounts. Others drink six glasses a day, but my doctor has ordered me to take only three. Not long ago I read in Frankel's book that the water here, among its other properties, "disposes one toward intellectual and spiritual activity." So that's the secret. Add to that the wonderful air, exercise until five each day, a stable diet, and not a trace of wine or vodka, and you'll understand how something that didn't get written in eight years wrote itself in one month. My suitcase has now taken on greater significance for me: I used to watch nonchalantly as it was thrown between train cars; now, however, I'll be following this procedure with anxiety. I informed Iuninka first that my time here hasn't been wasted, since she wanted this more than anyone – even more than I. She was so warm in her parting words, even made the sign of the cross over me. If I knew that I could finish the rest, I would just stay in some remote corner of Switzerland and not go to Paris. But I'm afraid that I won't finish it – after all, I am going to miss the Marienbad water when it's gone. The action is already taking place on [Petersburg's] Vyborg side; I have to describe this Vyborg Oblomovka, the hero's last love affair, his friend's futile effort to rouse him. Perhaps all this will fit into several scenes. Then it's three cheers for Goncharov! It is not so much the hope for another success that gladdens me as it is the thought that I will be rid of this burden on my soul, this yoke of duty and obligation I have been carrying on my shoulders. May God grant it!

TO S. A. NIKITENKO[6]

Marienbad, 15 August 1857

. . . I stayed on in Marienbad ten days after my treatment ended in order to finish all of *Oblomov* – and I did it! This was also a treatment of sorts, and I don't know which results will be better – perhaps neither one. But I have done everything humanly possible. In less than two months I've written sixty-two pages, and still have to finish the last two scenes – the final farewell of Oblomov and his friend, and a short conclusion where I'll tell what becomes of all the main characters in the novel. The scenes are already in draft form and could be finished in three or four sittings. But a couple of days ago the intensity of my writing made me ill . . . [so] I packed up the manuscript in my suitcase until Paris or Petersburg. There's still a mountain of work: first, I have to refine certain characters and scenes – even though many of them simply poured out of me and won't require much effort, and others I've managed to work on here. Then I have to decide if all this is any good, and if so, *how* good. I cannot make this determination on my own, and need my friends' advice – yours, of course, more than anyone else's. I am afraid of one thing: what if, say, you resent the thought of being my tutor and refuse? In that case, just remember that many stupid mistakes you might have prevented will get into print. . . .

I've been so immersed in my work that I've written more in the last two months than any other man would have in two lifetimes. Now I am craving some peace and quiet . . .

TO IU. D. EFREMOVA

Dresden, 11 September 1857

. . . The reason I didn't go to Switzerland is simple: laziness. . . . I'd rather just lie on my couch. I'm tired of unpacking, packing, rushing, and haven't the slightest curiosity about anything: I don't care at this point whether I see another sight or not. Your hopes that a trip abroad would revive me, that I would snap out of my melancholy and write the whole time (since you say writing is my calling and all that) – these hopes were in vain. Just because I've written a novel that had been in my head for a long time doesn't mean that I can write anything else. I'd been living with that novel for ten years, ever since I was a young man – I couldn't possibly have thought up everything there all at once. Besides, I can say honestly and without the slightest affectation that the novel is not nearly as good as could have been expected from me judging by my previous work. It's cold, listless, and strongly smacks of an assigned project. Perhaps if I had had six months to work on refining it I might have improved it somewhat, but as it is I'll just have to lump it together somehow. My melancholy follows me everywhere, and now it's no longer even melancholy but old age. What do you want from me: rejuvenation and blossoming? You are not suggesting I should marry, are you? Melancholy and peevishness are only the natural consequences of one's life experience and advanced years . . .

TO I. I. LKHOVSKY

Petersburg, 17 September 1858

. . . Thank you again for your suggestions for the novel. Many of them were invaluable and I followed them to the letter – all, that is, except the major ones, for which I have no energy. Also, I rewrote the "Stolz and Olga in Paris" chapter, which seemed as awkward to my listeners as it did to you . . .

TO I. I. LKHOVSKY

Petersburg, 5 November 1858

I recently read a highly favorable review of *The Frigate Pallas* in *Athenaeum*, where the author shows how foolish it is to invent literature especially for *children* when it already exists and is readily available in literature written for *adults* – and cites as examples Aksakov's *Childhood Years of Bagrov Grandson*, Turgenev's *Bezhin Meadow*, "Oblomov's Dream," *The Frigate Pallas*, and something of Grigorovich's. . . .

Now I am enjoying my last month of freedom: in December they'll begin copyediting . . . the first part of *Oblomov*. Recently I sat down to reread the latter and was horrified. In the last ten years I haven't read anything worse, weaker or paler than the first half of part 1: it's awful! I spent the next several days in a row shoveling out the muck, and there's still a good deal of it left! Reading the final scene between Oblomov and his servant, I was struck by the same thought you were; oh, if only others would understand it this way!

TO L. N. TOLSTOY

Petersburg, 4 December 1858

Most gracious and esteemed Lev Nikolaevich,

I arrived at Maikov's as he was finishing this letter, and requested a bit of space in which to recall myself to you and remind you of your promise that you would come to Petersburg and bring a little something new with you. We are all expecting you – and from you – very much. . . . As always, you are sorely missed here, your name uttered at every gathering as if part of the roll call. We're expecting many changes in literary censorship, but I am not going to describe them – the sooner, perhaps, you will be moved to come here. . . . Oh, Lev Nikolaevich, how we need the addition of your voice to current literature! . . . The year 1859 promises a kind of renewed refinement in taste; may God grant it be a happy one not for the peasants alone.[7] . . . I have [a] request for you: . . . Do not read the first part of *Oblomov;* if you have time, however, please do read the second and third, which were written much later. Part 1, on the other hand, was written in 1849 and is no good.

TO L. N. TOLSTOY

Petersburg, 13 May 1859

Count Lev Nikolaevich, I have been meaning for a long time to say a warm thank you for your kind words concerning *Oblomov,* which ricocheted back to me in a letter from Alexander Vasil'evich [Druzhinin]. . . . I value your words about my novel all the more for knowing how demanding and sometimes even fickle you can be when it comes to literary taste and judgment. . . . In short, you are not easy to please, and this made it especially gratifying to gain in you a champion of my new work. It would be even more gratifying if your words hadn't ricocheted to me, but if you had told me directly – about my lapses, about the things that didn't work to the novel's advantage, too. This would be particularly useful to me now since I would like to try, once again, my pen at something I've had in mind for a long time [i. e., *The Precipice*]. . . .

TO P. V. ANNENKOV[8]

Petersburg, 20 May 1859

. . . Are you getting any journals? Please have a look at Dobrolyubov's article on *Oblomov*. It seems to me that after this there's nothing left to say on the topic of what "Oblomovitis" is. No doubt he foresaw this and rushed to get his article into print before anyone else. He amazed me with two of his observations: he has a keen awareness of the artist's creative process. How could he possibly know this, not being an artist himself? . . . I did not expect such sympathy, such a sensitive reading from him – I had judged him to be much dryer. But perhaps I'm biased in his favor now, since the article as a whole is very good for me.

In spite of all this, I'd still like to see *your* review of the novel . . . – you have a uniquely subtle approach, and, what is more, your articles do not have a formal, journalistic air. . . . It is not as though I would count on your resounding approval, since you gave the novel the coldest reception of anyone to whom I read it. I would like your critique because you always manage to notice something that evades others. Besides, I have been listening eagerly to *all* the responses to my novel, good or bad, useful or useless, because I myself still do not have a clear sense of what I have written.

TO I. I. LKHOVSKY

St. Petersburg, 20 May 1859

. . . Now that all four parts of *Oblomov* have come out, it has made a bigger splash than either you or I expected. The public has echoed your fondness for the novel – only far more loudly. Even people who are not especially well disposed toward me share the positive impression. It's huge and unanimous. Dobrolyubov wrote an excellent article for *The Contemporary* in which he analyzes "Oblomovitis" fully and in detail. I'm pleased to tell you that no response to the novel, either in person or in print, has exceeded the scope of your assessment – they all turn on it, directly or indirectly. What a loss it is for me that you are not here. Now you could have given free rein to your pen without fear of reproach for being biased. In short: I'm the star of the show at the moment. There is only one aspect of it that's uncomfortable: many people want to make my acquaintance, and, what is more, everyone I meet immediately starts talking about [the novel]. Of course, when the fervor cools down, people will start to criticize me as well, especially in Moscow – even though the first two parts were greeted there with the same enthusiasm. But Moscow is the home of the Slavophiles, and Stolz is German.

TO S. A. NIKITENKO

Boulogne, Tuesday, 16 August 1860

. . . Now I'll say a word or two about your anxieties – the fear that the sky is falling, followed by the sudden drunken feeling, then the ecstasy, then the dejection, and so on. These are your life forces at work. Remember how I alluded to this in Olga's character: she also experienced a violent physical upheaval as a result of her burgeoning love for Oblomov. It is part of human nature, at a certain time, to be awakened by the fire of existence, to demand room to move, to crave the pleasure of action (yes, yes: the happiness that comes from fulfilling a desire to act is a kind of pleasure!). These attacks are the fever of being alive; one need only understand this fact – that is, adjust one's behavior according to one's awareness of it, tame it by knowing what it is (my Olga says, "*I know* it's just my nerves, the forces of nature at work!") – in order to remain in control of one's perception and impressions, and of the feelings responsible for them. One thus remains in control of *oneself*, preserves the integrity of one's consciousness, knows what to do and how to behave. Our grandmothers and even our mothers . . . didn't know this and called it *vaguement*, exaltation. They were at a loss, thought it was some kind of cruel affliction, became distant, gazed at the moon, cried; . . . some even lost their minds. Here is where analysis comes in handy. All this is really nothing more than life forces manifesting themselves. It is a kind of steam, if you will, that one should not let escape indiscriminately – or let suffocate one – but rather should put to use moving the train along the rails, should apply to reading, writing, whatever one is supposed to do. I think I understand and can explain these outbursts on the basis of personal experience: they have affected me as well, and, like our grandmothers, I have lost myself in daydreaming and flights of fancy when my nature was telling me to "work, think, do!" Instead I climbed the walls, gazed at the moon, and if I were not so fat I probably would have cried and, who knows, even lost my mind. But I was rescued partly by a weakness for life's pleasures, and partly by savvy.

Now: about those internal contradictions that cause you such bafflement on my account. . . . There is, I hope, a difference between the apathy of the fat, pampered aristocrat and that of a man who has all his life been attended by conscious thought, feelings, and material hardships. It should also be said that there resides in me the capacity of injecting a joke into it all. Sometimes I have found humor in things that others take very seriously . . .

TO S. A. NIKITENKO

Berlin, 30 May 1868

. . . You know who you are to me, Sofya Aleksandrovna? Agafya Matveyevna! Please don't be offended – I'll explain everything. (I am planning to insert at the end of the novel two words you spoke – only two, but they are very dear to me.) I'll tell you now what kind of Agafya Matveyevna you are for me . . .

You are the enviable Agafya Matveyevna, my moral custodian. Did you know that whenever I notice some worthless trait in myself, I ask myself, "Now what would Sofya Aleksandrovna have said, what kind of look would she have given me?" And I run straight to you to tell you when something is wrong. . . . You and I also share intellectual interests. . . . I should add that during the several days when she was listening to me read from my notebooks, Countess Tolstaya, also, suddenly became Agafya Matveyevna for me. But she already has her own Oblomov. . . . Nevertheless, she was generous enough to throw a crumb or two my way. . . . These crumbs were like diamonds to me. . . .

TO S. A. NIKITENKO

Bad Schwalbach, 4 July 1868

. . . On the subject of translations, yesterday Stasiulevich pointed out a recently published German edition of *Oblomov* in a bookstore window. I cannot stand to see myself translated; I write for Russians, and attention from foreigners is not the least bit flattering to me. We have no copyright agreements with Germany – I would not have permitted this otherwise.

TO S. A. NIKITENKO

Paris, 24 July 1869

. . . Madame Léo [the author of the newly published novel *Aline Ali*] is a *penseuse*, a lady philosopher who lacks the knowledge to support her opinions – and thus shakes on her foundations. Artistry might have helped her, if only she had been able faithfully to illuminate with her paintbrush, with the vital torch of art, those depths that her thought cannot reach; alas, however, she has almost no talent. Her writing is dull, listless, practically unreadable. . . .

What kind of perverted, sick imagination would allow one to dress up as a young boy and throw oneself at a handsome man's feet (remember that extremely distasteful scene where they have fallen into a ditch in the snow, and she is swooning in his passionate embrace?), only to recoil in horror at these same caresses when back in a woman's dress! . . .

But the author – or, more accurately, her heroine – admits that by renouncing her status and calling as a woman, with all its rights and responsibilities, she has gone too far, has crossed into the realm of ideals that humans cannot hope to attain. This is why, emerging from her ravings, she rushes off in pursuit of the lover she has just spurned for some reason utterly contrary to human nature. . . . She is a madwoman, and the book with her story is a dangerous one! Though it does contain excellent and true passages where she protests against male lechery, brute domination, and all the rest of it, yet how one-sided the book is, how superficial and ignorant of all aspects of life's experience!

To answer such enormous questions as who is to blame, men or women, for the hideous, chaotic state of relations between the sexes, for their positions in the family and in society at large, for the roles assigned each, and, finally, for the crippled psychologies of both – to answer these questions, even to utter the slightest peep about them, is practically impossible, you see, before the sciences – through experimentation, observation, and all those things – offer us theories about the natures, talents, and abilities of this or that sex, about their differences and similarities, and ultimately about human nature in general, that are at least somewhat more conclusive than those offered thus far. After all, it hasn't even been decided yet whether man is just another animal or something more than that, whether he has a dual nature, and so on.

But given that nobody has positive answers to these questions, and that some of these answers may forever remain unknown, there is no point in getting angry and climbing up on some superhuman pedestal. What both sexes *should* do is try to improve themselves a little, be a bit more honest and clearheaded, restrain a bit their animal outbursts. We should extend our hands to each other *à l'amiable*, acknowledge to one another as friends our mutual nastiness, and be simply, honestly, straightforwardly, human beings – then we can decide *à l'amiable* what women can do and men cannot, and vice versa. Now we're talking! If that woman with all her grand visions had changed not her nature (for this is impossible) but her habits, perverse ideas, and false principles concerning her Paolo, had acknowledged that women, in their turn, have also been poisoned by nastiness (each sex has poisoned the other), had yielded to him for love's sake and because he had behaved honorably, and had thus provided society with an example of a harmonious marriage – *then* people might have believed and approved of her more. But she placed her squeamishness, her narrow, dried-up, proud little ego on a level higher than that of her calling and purpose as a woman and as a person – and lost herself in the clouds, in her preposterous self-imposed loneliness.

Devoted herself to charity! What she does is not true charity – that comes only from the heart. And just imagine what a rich and vital reservoir it might have been, the love – tender, passionate, all-encompassing – that might have flowed thence had she been noble and happy, had she not glued her eyes shut with her monasticism, her biblical morals. Simply a kind and honorable person can sometimes do more good without spending a single ruble than a philanthropist who sits on the boards of many charities but is indifferent to real people.

Only a warm, loving person creates around herself a radiant aura of happiness – not just from visiting hospitals or organizing schools but because whatever her kind, winning nature touches becomes easy, straightforward, pure. *She* becomes a nun, says, "I want no part of this filthy, depraved world, and turn my back on it for my own salvation!" Nuns and monks are egoists who will be locked up in their isolation even in the kingdom of Heaven; there they'll be told, "You can live by and for yourselves in paradise, too, since you did not want to help others, did not know how to save yourselves among them."

Good deeds done according to lists, schedules, and statistical tables belong to the realms of organized charity and government. Of course each individual member of a charity makes his own contribution – as one would pay a tax – but all these organizations are at the level of state and society, where people make determinations about the nature of human needs and the amount of aid required to satisfy them, not with the heart but with the mind, by conscious reason. This is a public service, but it has little to do with the private, personal pleasure of helping someone directly; of extending one's hand to a poor or sick person and, in becoming a friend to him, gaining a friend yourself; of the reward of witnessing firsthand how kindness turns evil to good, poverty to abundance, sickness to health.

Just ask people who love flowers. They will tell you what a difference there is between hiring a gardener, between seeing flowers at a market or a public garden, and growing and caring for them yourself.

Well, you know all this better than I and better than any Aline Ali; you always find friends among those you help out, because besides simply helping them, you also love them. This is what true charity is all about.

As regards the debate about who is to blame, men or women, who corrupted whom, who's worse, who's better – it is pointless and impractical, and is starting to sound silly. It would be better for men and women to begin improving themselves rather than to argue about who is to blame for what, about who spoiled everything. . . .

TO S. A. NIKITENKO

Petersburg, 25 February 1873
. . . People think years alone make one old, when really it's one's nature, way of life, and individual circumstances!

I tried to show in *Oblomov* how and why our people turn to mush before their time: the landscape and climate, the vast distances and isolation, a soporific lifestyle – as well as those situations unique to each person. What can one do?

TO A. A. TOLSTAYA[9]

Petersburg, 14 April 1874
. . . Countess Tolstaya, you once remarked very astutely that my social reticence most likely conceals vanity. This may be so, but what of it? What is the point in trying to conquer my shyness? So I can show my face all over town? Once again I ask: Why? Others have little need for my company, and, now that I am old, I myself have few needs. At the same time, I do not wish to appear strange or awkward. So you are right: I am vain, too. "Oh, you're just an Oblomov!" is the usual response to my reclusion.

Eh bien, après? That's right, I *am* an Oblomov – but unlike all the other Oblomovs of this world.

It is not just laziness, not just an aversion to new experience, or other simplistic outside factors that have kept me at a distance from those blandishments of high society I find so unenticing. What about my artistic spirit, the spirit of poetry, and all those other things that shun the public eye or *gêne* of any kind, that demand all sorts of minor freedoms, and so on? In short, what about the internal factors?

Just think what I've been through! I have always wanted to *write* – it is my calling – but was forced into the civil service. I am nervous, an impressionable and irritable creature who needs clear fresh air and sunshine, some peace and quiet. For forty years, though, I have been living in a fog under a leaden sky, have hardly been able to scrape together one month a year to do what I want to do, what I *should* be doing. Instead I have always done that for which I have neither desire nor talent.

On Thursday I also said I would not write anymore. This is probably the case, though my heart bleeds because of it.

TO THÉODORE DE VIZEVÁ[10]

1880s

. . . I have never believed in the so-called immortality of literary works. In the past, when literary production was smaller, a single book might well have kept its value for twenty years or more. But even during those times literary value was only relative: subsequent generations might still have marveled at the writer's talent, even though they had in fact ceased to understand him . . .

Thank God that in my time I have enjoyed the success I deserved and more. Now my works have grown old like myself. Any attempt to represent them — or me — as still youthful is just the sort of vanity I am trying to steer clear of. This is why I have done my best to prevent their republication in my homeland, and it would be regrettable to learn that there are people in some foreign country who wish to exhume them from the grave . . .

TO V. V. STASOV[11]

Petersburg, 17 August 1882
Dear Vladimir Vasil'evich,

In response to your inquiry, I hasten to inform you that of all my novels I believe only *Oblomov* has been translated into German – by whom I do not know. I happened to see this translation twelve years ago, in a bookstore window somewhere in Germany.

I should add that I have been approached many times – among others, by someone in Petersburg – for permission to translate my other novels as well, especially *The Precipice*. I have given everyone the same answer: that I consider an author's giving his "permission" for a translation extremely immodest, and at the same time can claim no right to forbid it. I therefore counsel the gentlemen to act as they see fit as concerns the translation of my works.

In general, I think that translations of Russian works voicing peculiarly *national* concerns little known outside this country will not be of much interest to European readers. Thus, for example, Oblomov and others like him will appear to them incomprehensible and hardly entertaining. For this reason I am quite ambivalent about attempts to convey Russian writers into foreign languages.

TO A. F. KONI[12]

Petersburg, 11 November 1882
. . . Your reading *Oblomov* is very consoling to me; I had thought that it – along with all books as old as it is – was unreadable. Well, it's not my problem now. I didn't force my copyright on them – they badgered me until I gave it up. If they don't turn a profit, then they have only themselves to blame.

Also, I have had – am having even now – to fight a battle of sorts with Mikhail Matveevich about some sinister plans he has for celebrating my fiftieth "anniversary." . . . [A]t dinner, I called attention to the curious coincidence that this year marks, first, my seventieth birthday; second, fifty years since 1832, when I published my fragment of a French novel in *The Telescope* [i. e., Sue's *Atar-Gull*], and third, thirty-five years since 1847, when *A Common Story* appeared in *The Contemporary*. . . . I also requested that you not tell anyone about these anniversaries lest they are leaked to the press. I do not want any fanfare. . . . None at all!

TO V. V. STASOV

Petersburg, 27 October 1888
Dear Vladimir Vasil'evich,

You have been so forceful in your declarations that you would like from me some draft manuscripts of my published work for preservation in the National Public Library that, after protesting fairly vigorously, I am finally giving in. "Don't argue with Stasov," Turgenev maintains, while Count Tolstoy has been instructing me not to "resist evil." I am not arguing anymore because, among other reasons, I am not a strong enough opponent. . . . I am not "fighting evil" either, since I do not see anything particularly evil in your request – save only that I do not fully understand the reason behind it. Indeed, it is quite difficult to refuse: this would be the equivalent of refusing to give you some old and threadbare clothes. . . . Don't they amount to the same thing? Once Professor Nikitenko, who has been dead for years, suggested to me that I submit a manuscript to the public library. When I asked why in surprise, he was unable to offer a definite answer.

Krylov, Pushkin, Griboedov, Lermontov, and other torch bearers who broke new literary ground, the great pioneers of Russian culture – their manuscripts are a different matter. . . .

Be this as it may, I am nevertheless fulfilling your desire; I am even attaching in addition a small portrait to go with the manuscripts, as per your request. All this I grant on one firm condition: that my letter to you be kept with the manuscripts themselves, *as proof that I did not come knocking on the library doors out of pride, manuscripts pretentiously in hand, but rather was impelled to do so by you*

– who, as the librarian, no doubt partly represents the library itself. If in time the presence of my manuscripts there comes to be viewed as inappropriate, I do not wish responsibility to fall on me.

I attach herewith the following:

1. A handwritten draft manuscript of *Oblomov* in its entirety, with the exception of "Oblomov's Dream." That chapter was published as a fragment in *The Contemporary* in 1848 or 1849, I don't remember which, and was probably removed from the draft manuscript for that reason. Of course, that the whole manuscript underwent radical changes before it was published is obvious from the corrections and innumerable alterations on each page. Incidentally, in the draft of the first part there is a kind of introductory character, one Pochaev, who disappears in part 2 and does not appear in the final published version.

Oblomov was begun in 1846, after I had submitted my first novel, *A Common Story*, to the editors at *The Contemporary*. When I had finished the first part, I set it aside and did not touch it again until 1857. During the intervening years I sailed around the world, taking the first part of *Oblomov* with me but not working on it. Rather, I was thinking over and planning in my head another novel, *The Precipice*, initially conceived in 1849 on the Volga, where I spent that summer.

It was already 1857 when I traveled to the waters at Marienbad and finished the second, third, and fourth parts of Oblomov in one long sitting. I stayed there around two months – beyond my allotted time – and wrote only the novel's final chapters the following winter in Petersburg. There you have the history of the writing of *Oblomov*. . . .

NOTES

1. Andrey Aleksandrovich Kraevsky (1810–1889) was at the time the publisher and editor of *Otechesvennye zapiski* (National annals), to which *Oblomov* was "promised" and which would publish it ten years later.

2. Elizaveta Vasil'evna Tolstaya (1829–1877) was, as mentioned in the

introduction, a friend of the Maikovs and a subject of Goncharov's strong attachment in the mid-1850s on his return from the *Frigate Pallas* voyage. She married Alexander Musin-Pushkin in 1857.

3. One of the competing journals was *Sovremennik* (The contemporary), which prior to that point had published all other Goncharov's fictional works, including "Oblomov's Dream." Nekrasov, who was still the editor, was thus hoping that Goncharov would place the entire *Oblomov* with him. By 1859, however, *Sovremennik*, which recently had added to its staff both Chernyshevsky and Dobrolyubov, was becoming too radical not just for Goncharov but also for Turgenev and Tolstoy, who preferred to place their work elsewhere. The journal's increasingly radical nature became quite obvious in the early 1860s when *Sovremennik* published Chernyshevsky's *What Is to Be Done?* and Nekrasov's harsh poetic condemnations of the tsarist government. Consequently it was suspended by Alexander II in 1866, despite Nekrasov's attempts to placate the ruler at the last moment. For more on *Sovremennik*'s radicalization and demise, see, among others, Avdotya Panaeva, *Vospomonaniia* (Memoirs) (Moscow: Pravda, 1986), pp. 285–379.

4. Ivan Ivanovich Lkhovsky (1829–1867) also worked for the Ministry of Finances and was one of Goncharov's closest friends. Goncharov served in many ways as the mentor for Lkhovsky who had writing ambitions of his own. In 1859 he even followed in Goncharov's footsteps and took a round-the-world voyage.

5. Iunya Dmitrievna Efremova (no dates available), was niece of Ekaterina Maikova and, together with her aunt and Sofya Nikitenko, among the closest of Goncharov's female friends.

6. Sofya Aleksandrovna Nikitenko (1840–1901), a daughter of Alexander Nikitenko, professor of literature at Petersburg University and Goncharov's fellow censor. Sofya Nikitenko was a professional translator and often helped Goncharov with his manuscripts.

7. There was much talk at the time about the liberation of serfs occasioned by the establishment that year of gentry committees in all Russian provinces to study the question of emancipation. Alexander II, who succeeded his father in 1855, signed the official manifesto liberating the serfs in 1861. (For more on that, see Nicholas V. Riasanovsky, *A History of Russia* [New York: Oxford University Press, 1963], pp. 408–15).

8. Pavel Vasil'evich Annenkov (1813–1887) was a critic, a biographer of Pushkin, and a close friend of Turgenev.

9. Countess Alexandra Andreevna Tolstaya (1817–1904) was one of the empress's ladies in waiting, as well as Leo Tolstoy's aunt.

10. Théodore de Vizevá (no dates available) was a French literary critic who wanted to popularize Goncharov's work in France.

11. Vladimir Vladimirovich Stasov (1824–1906) worked at the time as the art librarian at St. Petersburg Public Library. He was a renowned art specialist and critic.

12. Anatoly Fedorovich Koni (1844–1927) became Goncharov's closest friend in the last twenty years of the writer's life. Koni was a prominent lawyer and an acclaimed memoirist.

Miscellaneous Prose

Translated from the Russian by
BRIAN THOMAS OLES

A Cruel Affliction (1838) (Excerpt)

The other character is my school friend, Nikon Ustinovich Tiazhelenko, a Ukrainian landowner and also an old friend of the Zurovs. It is he who introduced us. He had been well known since childhood for his unparalleled, methodical laziness, and a heroic indifference to worldly concerns. He spent most of his life lying in bed, and if he did ever sit up it was only at the dinner table. In his opinion, it was not worth sitting up for breakfast and supper. As I mentioned, he left the house rarely and, as a result of such a sedentary life, had acquired all the attributes of a sloth. His deliberately large and thriving paunch rose up like a mountain. Folds cascaded along his whole body as on a rhinoceros, creating a sort of natural clothing. Though he lived near the Tauride Gardens, to go for a walk there was for him a heroic act. His doctors predicted a whole battery of illnesses and various deaths for him, but to no avail: he countered all their objections with the simplest and most logical of arguments. For example, if they chastised him for not walking very much and warned that he might contract apoplexy, he replied that he walked down the corridor leading from his front door to his bedroom at least five times a day, which in his opinion was more than enough to prevent a stroke. And he would add the following remark in conclusion: should he, Tiazhelenko, have a stroke, it would provide a legitimate excuse to stay at home all the time, would serve as an eloquent defense against all the doctors' reproaches – and then there would be no point in worrying about his health anyway. As for the fresh air of which they recommended he partake, he maintained that on awaking in the morning he would put his face up to an open window and suck in enough air to last him the whole day. Doctors and friends shrugged their shoulders and left him alone. This is my friend Nikon Ustinovich. He liked the Zurovs and visited them once a month, but as he found this more than he could handle, he purposely introduced me to them. "Drop in on them often, my friend," he said to me. "They're wonderful people. I love them terribly, but they insist that I visit them once a week. Can you believe it?! So: *you* please visit them and tell them what's happening with me, and me what's happening with them."

Thus it was he I set out to visit on noticing something strange at the Zurovs', in hopes that, as an old friend of theirs who knew everything about them, he would be able to provide me with an explanation. At the moment I dropped in, he was contemplating turning onto his left side.

"Hello, Nikon Ustinovich!" I said. He nodded from a reclining position. "Are you well?" Once again he nodded in affirmation: Nikon Ustinovich did not care to waste words. "The Zurovs send their regards and chide you for not liking them anymore." He shook his head in dissent. "Won't you please say something, my dear friend?"

"There . . . wait . . . let me get going here," he finally enounced slowly. "They're about to serve breakfast, so I guess I'll sit up."

Five minutes later the servant managed with great effort to haul to the table what Nikon Ustinovich modestly called "my breakfast," and what four other people could easily call their own. A side of beef barely fit on the plate, and the edges of the tray were adorned with eggs. Next, there was a cup – or, I think, more like a bowl – of hot chocolate steaming like a riverboat, and finally a bottle of porter towering over everything else.

"There now, I – " Tiazhelenko began both to speak and sit up but managed to do neither and fell back onto the pillow.

"Do you really eat all that by yourself?"

"No, I give some to the dog," he answered, pointing at a tiny, immobile lap dog that, like him, lay in the same spot, evidently to please its master.

"Well, may God be your judge! But jokes aside," I continued, "won't you go to the Zurovs' for dinner with me?"

"Ah! What? Are you in your right mind?" he said, waving his arm. "Why don't you stay with me, dear chap? I'm having some wonderful ham, sturgeon, Siberian pelmeni, sausages, pudding, turkey, and a wonderful soufflé. I gave the cooking instructions myself."

"No, thank you. I gave my word – besides, they're going to have an interesting conversation at the table today about preparations for their walks in the country."

Suddenly Tiazhelenko's face came to life. He made a terrible effort and – sat up.

"You, too! You, too!" we both shouted simultaneously.

"What does your exclamation mean?" I asked.

"And yours?"

"Mine," I answered, "came out of surprise: recently Zurov went into convulsions, and now you nearly got up on your feet merely from my having mentioned spring walks in the country. So you see my cry was not without reason. What about you, though?"

"My reason is more important," he answered depositing a piece of roast beef in his mouth. "I thought you were ill."

"Ill? Thank you for your concern. But where did you get that idea?"

"I thought that . . . you might have caught something. . . . "

"This is going from bad to worse! From whom? What?"

"From whom? From the Zurovs."

"How absurd! Explain yourself, please!"

"Wait a minute! Let me . . . eat something first." And he chewed on the meat quietly, slowly, like a cow. Finally the last piece disappeared; everything had been eaten and drunk, and the servant who had carried the breakfast in with both hands carried the remains out with two fingers. I moved closer and Tiazhelenko began:

"Have you noticed anything in particular about the Zurovs in the three years you have known them?"

"Not up to now."

"Are you going to the country this summer?"

"No, I'm staying here."

"In that case, starting this morning you will start noticing strange things on a daily basis."

"What on earth is the meaning of this? Will you tell me already? And if there was something special about them, why didn't you mention it before?"

"Hmm, the thing is – " slowly continued Tiazhelenko, "the Zurovs are suffering from an illness."

"What illness are you talking about?" I yelled, terrified.

"A very strange one, my friend, very strange – and very contagious. Sit down, listen, and don't rush me. . . . I can see that I will be dead tired today as it is. It's no laughing matter, having to talk so much. But it can't be helped: I have to save you. I haven't told you until now because there was no reason to: you lived in Petersburg only in the winter, and one can't notice anything in them then. They have worlds of knowledge, and time flies unnoticed in conversation with them. But in the summer, it's amazing! They aren't themselves, they're completely different people. They don't eat, they don't drink, they have only one thing on their minds . . . Complaints! Complaints! And there is no way to help them!"

"At least tell me the name of this disease and what the symptoms are!" I demanded.

"It has no name, because evidently this is the first case. But I will describe the symptoms. How, where should I start? . . . You see . . . It's a very complicated thing when there's no name for it . . . Well, let me refer to it simply as a 'cruel affliction,' at least for the time being. When the doctors figure it out, let them christen it with their own name. The thing is that in the summer the Zurovs just cannot stay at home – that's how terrible, how deadly an illness it is." And Tiazhelenko let out half a pound of air in one breath and made a most sour grimace, as though having some tasty morsel wrested from his teeth. I started laughing.

"Forgive me, Nikon Ustinych! This is an illness in your eyes only.

You're consumed with a far more dangerous disease, spending your whole life lying in one place. Your extreme behavior will lead to death far more quickly than the Zurovs'. Or perhaps you are joking?"

"Some joke! It's a disease, my friend, a terrible disease! I'll explain it once again more clearly: they are being destroyed by an indomitable passion for walks in the country!"

"But that is a most pleasant passion! I gave them my word I myself would join them on their trips to the country."

"You gave them your word?" he exclaimed. "Oh, poor Fillip Klimych! What have you done? You're doomed!" He almost began to cry. "Have you already spoken about this to Verenitsyn?"

"Not yet."

"Thank God! There is still time to put things right, but you have to do as I tell you." I looked at him perplexedly. He continued, "I remember in the old days when I was dumb enough to spend most of the day on my feet (there's youth for you!) I used not to be averse to going into the forest with a few provisions in hand, say a turkey and a bottle of Malaga in my pocket. I would sit under a tree on a warm day, eat, then lie down on the grass. And then, well – back home again. But these people are killing themselves with walks. Imagine how far they've gone! In the summer, if they do stay home on any day – and I overheard them admit as much during one of their bouts of illness – it is because something is weighing on them, tormenting them, won't leave them in peace. Some irresistible force draws them out of the city, an evil spirit enters them, and so they – " At this point Tiazhelenko's speech became more heated. " – they swim, hop, run – and when they've swum, jumped, and run all the way there, then they nearly walk themselves to death. I cannot understand why they don't keel over! They either climb up steep hills or climb down ravines." Here he accompanied each concept with a florid gesture. "They wade through streams, get stuck in swamps, force their way through thorny underbrush, and scramble up the highest trees. How many times they've nearly drowned, fallen into some crevasse, sunk into the mud, frozen and even – it's horrible! – endured hunger and thirst!"

Tiazhelenko exuded this whole peroration together with sweat. Oh, how magnificent he was at that moment! Righteous indignation was written on his ample brow, large drops of sweat poured down his forehead and cheeks – given the inspired expression on his face, one would be permitted mistaking them for tears. The classical, golden age of yore came to life before me; I searched for an appropriate comparison between Tiazhelenko and some famous historical figure, finally finding it in the similar persona of the Roman emperor Vitellius.

"Bravo! Bravissimo! Excellent!" I shouted as he continued:

"Yes, Fillip Klimych. Calamity, utter calamity has befallen them! Walking all day long! It's a good thing they at least sweat – this is what saves them. But soon even this bountiful dew will dry up and be gone, and then . . . what will become of them? The infection is now deeply rooted, it's slowly running through their blood vessels, consuming their vital essence. That kind Alexey Petrovich! That gracious Maria Aleksandrovna! The venerable grandmother! Those children, poor young people! Youth, blooming health, bright-eyed hopes – everything will languish, exhaust itself, and disappear – all from excruciating, self-imposed labor!" He covered his face with his hands, and I started laughing. "And you laugh, heartless!"

"How can I not laugh, my friend, when you, the most indifferent of people – so untroubled by life that if the whole world came crashing down over your head, you wouldn't even open your mouth to ask what all the noise was about – have been agonizing and perspiring for a whole hour; if you were able, you would even cry. And all because someone else is partaking of that pleasure which is most hateful to you – walking!"

"You still cannot grasp the fact that I am not joking. Haven't you seen the warning signs?" he said with vexation.

'I don't know. It seemed as if . . . But what are the signs?" I asked.

"Incessant yawning, pensiveness, melancholy, lack of sleep and appetite, pallor and at the same time weird spots all over the face. There's something wild and strange in their eyes."

"This is what I came to ask you about."

"Well then – you must understand and keep in mind that whenever they think of the forest, fields, swamps, or secluded places, all these symptoms appear. They are consumed by melancholy and the shivers until they satisfy their tragic desire. Then they rush out in a great hurry, without looking back, taking almost no basic necessities with them. It is as though they have been set off by something, are being chased by all the demons in Hell."

"So where is it they go?"

"Everywhere. There isn't a single bush within a thirty-mile radius of Petersburg they haven't poked around in. I am not talking about the famous places like Peterhof and Pargolovo, which everyone visits. These days they look for remote places rarely frequented by people, in order to – get this! – to converse with nature, breathe the fresh air, escape the dust, and . . . who knows what else! Listen to Maria Aleksandrovna, she'll tell you absolutely everything. "Here," she'll say, "you can suffocate even in the markets and restaurants!" Hm! What an injustice, what an extreme lack of appreciation for markets and restaurants, those refuges of health and worldly happiness! To run from the hub where nature's two richest kingdoms – the animal and the plant – are concentrated, to suffocate from the air in those places where palaces are erected and altars raised to that sweetest of necessities – *food*. Tell me, what public square is grander than the market square, and how is the exhibit of nature's creations held there any lesser than an art exhibit? Finally, to shun the only pleasure that does not shun us and is forever young, always fresh, daily lavishing us with new and undying flowers! Everything else is a phantom; everything is unstable, temporary. Other joys evade us at the very moment we are about to attain them. Here, on the other hand, if something were ever to think of evading us, a well-aimed bullet would fly on ahead, obeying our whim, and overpower the brazen creature. What's the point of other comforts and vast means if they are not used to enjoy and appreciate – "

Seeing that Tiazhelenko had got caught up in the finer points of gastronomy, a science he was perfecting in both theory and practice (and of which he had provided me two example in one morning), I stopped him. "You've forgotten about the Zurovs," I said.

"What else can I say about them? They are a lost family! Imagine – " he continued, "Alexey Petrovich's regular stroll encompasses a loop that nearly exceeds the sum total of all the walks I have taken in my whole life. For example, he might set off from Gorokhovaia Street toward the Nevsky Monastery, whence he would proceed to Kamennyi Island, then from Krestovsky Island past Koltovskaia to Petrovsky Island, from Petrovsky to Vasilievsky Island, and back to Gorokhovaia again. How do you like that? And all this is walking or running. Isn't that awful? And that's not all! Sometimes in the middle of the night, when everybody and everything lies sleeping, rich and poor, animals and . . . birds – "

"I don't think birds lie down to sleep," I noted.

"Yes – well, in any case. I feel sorry for them! Why should nature deny them this simple delight! Where was I just now?"

"You were talking about birds."

"But you say birds don't lie down. Wait – who else lies down to sleep?"

"Can't you just speak more simply, my dear Tiazhelenko? Stay closer to the matter at hand. Otherwise you'll tire yourself out."

"True, true. Thank you for reminding me. Allow me to lie down – it will be more comfortable for me that way." He lay down on the pillows and continued. "So, sometimes at night, all of a sudden Alexey Petrovich will leap up from his bed, go out on the balcony, then wake up his wife. "What a marvelous night, Maria Alekseevna! What do you say we go out?" And then, all of a sudden – their sleep just evaporates! The whole house jumps out of bed, dresses in a hurry, and runs off accompanied by their two most loyal servants – who, alas, are also afflicted with this plague. Or sometimes, and I have witnessed this myself, in the middle of dinner, at the most joyous point of our existence – between the soup and the main course, when the first pangs of hunger have passed, but when the anticipation of further delectation has not yet been blunted – suddenly Alexey Petrovich will exclaim: "What if we were to finish these pastries and the main course out of town somewhere?" Implementation follows immediately on the heels of this idea: the main course and the pastries fly off to a field somewhere, and I return home alone, with tears in my eyes. No follower of Mohammed has ever hastened to Mecca with such zeal, no old woman from Moscow or Kostroma ever craved so strongly the sacred air of the Kiev caves."

"With such an attraction to nature they should live in a dacha in a village," I said.

"They used to live there, but the children grew up. Concerns for their upbringing and other important circumstances keep them in the city. It would be fine if they bore the burden of this "cruel affliction" alone, but the problem is that many people solicit their acquaintance – the Zurovs are people of quality. And those who spend the summer here are doomed. The old professor has started to pine and is suffering from loss of appetite and insomnia. His niece Zinaida has lost several admirers who were not impressed with her new talent for – yawning. And the charming wife of the diplomat would meet a sorry fate if she didn't leave to take the waters every summer."

"It seems to me that you are the one suffering from an illness," I said. "I'm already hungry from listening to all your nonsense."

"I would never interfere with *that*," answered Tiazhelenko with displeasure, "just as I would never interfere in your decision whether or not to believe me."

"Don't be angry, my friend! Instead tell me how you intended to save me and what the root of this evil is."

"Oh! Haven't I told you yet? It's Verenitsyn, my friend: he's the cause of it all! He is the one who infected the Zurovs."

"Could that be? He seems very devoted to them – "

"Yes, yes," Nikon Ustinovich interrupted, "he is a good person, he likes to eat and everything, but what can you do! About eight years ago he set out to travel across Russia – he was in the Crimea, in

Siberia, in the Caucuses – the urge some people have to wander around the world! As if there's nothing to swallow here! Finally he retired to Orenburg District to live permanently. About four years ago, he returned here a changed man: he had the 'cruel affliction.' He visited the Zurovs every day as before, every day would slip a little poison into their minds, and finally poisoned them for good. Those who are close to him catch the illness faster, more easily, and more seriously."

"Well then," I asked, "have you inquired about the cause of his strange behavior?"

"Of course! I asked Verenitsyn himself, but he always answers incoherently, turns away in irritation, utters through his clenched teeth that "it's just a sickness!" Actually the Zurovs' housekeeper Anna Petrovna, who is a dear friend of mine, happened to tell me in confidence that while he was living in Orenburg District he would go out into the steppe quite often and fell in love with some Kalmyk or Tartar woman there. Who knows! You see what a man he is, you can't get a word out of him! Just try asking him sometime: "Ivan Stepanych, have you had dinner today? What did you have?" He won't tell you for anything. Most unforthcoming! Well – Anna Petrovna contends that he even lived in the *uluses* – the camps of nomadic tribes – and sired two children. Who knows where they've got to now. So is it any wonder that he acquired a partiality for fields while living in the steppe? There's nothing surprising in their allure: Asian wizards have always been more crafty than their European counterparts. Have you read what they say about the Arabian sorcerers? It's amazing! Perhaps the Kalmyk woman cast a spell on him out of jealousy. Stop by his place some evening: the condemned just sit there gazing into his eyes!"

"Who is condemned?"

"The kittens, the kittens! He has two of them at his bosom at all times, two sitting on the table and two on the bed – and during the day they all disappear. No matter how you look at it, there's something fishy going on!

"Aren't you ashamed, believing such nonsense?"

"I'm not saying I believe it; I'm just conveying Anna Petrovna's speculations."

"You still have not told me, however, how it is that you managed not to contract the illness yourself, and whether there is any way to prevent it."

"There is no established method, everyone has to make up his own. I was protected from the "cruel affliction" by the late colonel Trukhin, who also was not susceptible to it. He was a keen one, and as soon as Verenitsyn started casting the spell, he felt something unusual happening to him and used all his might to escape disaster. Fortunately he remembered some love poem that always made Verenitsyn weary. So the colonel started declaiming, and Verenitsyn fainted – thus he was saved. Since then Verenitsyn has made no attempts to destroy him, although he goes to great ends to ruin others. He creeps into your soul like a demonic tempter, puts you to sleep, drives you to a state of numbness, and then strikes with his spell – I don't know if it's something he gives you to eat or drink – so just when he set out to entangle me with his infernal net, I tried to think up some sort of *unusual* way to overwhelm him, which Trukhin strongly recommended. I thought and thought and finally – guess what I got him with?"

"I don't know," I answered.

"Do you remember my singing voice?"

"Your singing voice? What are you on about?"

"You really don't remember? Wait, I'll sing something – " He stretched his lips, filled his cheeks with air, and was about to shower the tabernacle with the most blasphemous of sounds when suddenly – I recalled that screeching of badly oiled wheels. My ears started to ache from the memory alone. I waved my arms and shouted at the top of my voice:

"I remember, I remember! For God's sake, don't start! Your voice is monstrous!"

"There you go!" he said. "Though my native land is famous for its melodic voices, I guess there has to be a black sheep in every flock!

Well, so just as soon as he started casting his spell on me, I suddenly began singing for all I was worth, and – he plugged his ears and stole away. You should think up something, too. Remember, though – you have to shock him right at the start, or you're done for! Later the Zurovs themselves decided to try to drag me into this, talked me into going for a walk with them to the Summer Gardens, probably with the intent of getting me to go out of town from there. It was no easy task extracting an agreement from me, but finally we went. On noticing their inimical designs, I started looking around for a place to hide. And would you believe it? There was a butcher just two steps away! There was nothing for it: they were engaged in conversation, and I dove into the shop. They simply couldn't guess where I'd got to and kept looking all around. I was peeking at them out the window and dying of laughter! Now that's all I can tell you of the "cruel affliction" – don't ask me anything more. Look at my face: you see how my serenity has been upset by the recollection of these bitter memories. Please understand the great sacrifice I am making for the sake of friendship. Go, stop disturbing my peace of mind. Hey Vorobenko!" he yelled to his servant, "bring me water to douse my head, draw the curtains, and don't disturb me until dinner."

I tried to ask him a few more questions but to no avail. He remained intractable, keeping a stubborn silence.

"Farewell, Nikon Ustinovich!"

He nodded his head silently, and we parted.

Better Late Than Never (1879) (Excerpts)

. . . I am referring to the curious processes of conscious versus unconscious creativity. Let me first state that I belong to the latter category, that is, I am easily carried away by "my ability to paint pictures," as Belinsky put it.

During the moments when I am painting, I can rarely tell what my image, portrait, or character means: I simply see it alive before my eyes and try to make certain my depiction is accurate. I see one character interacting with others, and from this I am able to depict

those other, new characters in scenes I visualize far ahead in the
novel – this before I even know how all the parts scattered in my
mind will come together. I rush to sketch scenes and characters on
sheets or even scraps of paper, before I forget them. I move on
almost blindly, and at first my writing is listless, clumsy, boring (like
the beginning of Oblomov and Raisky) and I am bored myself. Then
all of a sudden a flood of light illuminates the paths I should take. I
always have one image that serves as the main motif, that leads the
way – while I spontaneously grab whatever is at hand, i.e., that which
is closely related to this image, as I go. By now I am working ani-
matedly, cheerfully, my hand barely keeping up with my thoughts,
and so it goes until I hit the next brick wall. In the meantime I
continue to work in my head; the characters give me no respite, they
pester me, pose for scenes. I hear fragments of their conversations –
God help me, often it will seem to me that I am not making this up,
but that it is all floating in the air around me and I need only look
and listen carefully.

For example, the first image that struck me in regard to Oblomov
was laziness – which I saw in myself and in others – and it became
more and more vivid to me as I went along. Of course I instinctively
knew that little by little this character was absorbing the essential
traits of a Russian – and so far instinct has been sufficient for the
image to be true to Oblomov's character.

If I had been told at the time what Dobrolyubov and others – and,
finally, I myself – would see in him, I would have believed it, and
thus deliberately exaggerated one or another trait – ruining everything, of course. . . .

I will not dwell on *Oblomov*. In its time it was sensitively discussed
and its significance assessed both by the critics, particularly
Dobrolyubov, and by the public. They all found the embodiment of
sleep, stagnation, of a motionless, dead life – *of crawling from one day
to another* – in one character and his surroundings believable, and I
am pleased.

I had finished my second depiction of Russian life, "The Slumber," without rousing the main character – Oblomov himself.

Only Stolz would from time to time hold up before Oblomov a mirror reflecting his unfathomable laziness, apathy, and sleep. Together with Olga, he spent all his energy in order to rouse him – all in vain. It is only during his last meeting with Stolz that a few conscious words force their way out of Oblomov – and I was wrong to include even these. I put them in at the end, when an acquaintance of mine who is always hunting for conscious thoughts in a work of art, but who is not very perceptive when it comes to the actions themselves of the character, asked, "Isn't he going to respond to Stolz's appeals?"

So I put in a few words that reveal Oblomov's consciousness, and his whole image was somehow affected. Somehow his personality lost its wholeness; his portrait turned out blemished. Luckily, however, this was at the very end. I shouldn't have touched anything. It is no wonder that Belinsky reproached me in his review of *A Common Story* for "taking the path of conscious thought"! I should stick to images, convey meaning through them.

As Stolz leaves for the last time, he says tearfully, "Farewell, old Oblomovka! Your time has passed!"

I shouldn't even have said that. Oblomov is self-explanatory enough when he asks Stolz to leave, not to touch him, saying that *he is rooted by his sick half in the Old World. To pull it up would mean death!*

It is with such a deep sleep that I should have ended my second canvas, "The Slumber" – for just beyond the mountain of Oblomov's paunch (an expression Herzen coined somewhere in *The Bell*), a distant, third expanse opened up before me: the canvas of "The Awakening." . . .

Before I move on to *The Precipice*, I will say a few words about Stolz in *Oblomov*.

I have been taken to task for this character – and, on the one hand, rightly so. He is weak and pale, the idea behind him too naked. I am aware of this myself. But I have also been reproachfully asked why I put him in the novel at all. Why use a German rather than a Russian to contrast with Oblomov?

I could answer that after depicting laziness and congenital apathy, in all their various aspects, as elemental traits of Russians and no one else, I would, by placing another Russian next to Oblomov as a model of energy, knowledge, and hard work – of strength in general – have stumbled into a kind of contradiction with myself, that is, with my goal of depicting stagnation, sleep, and immobility. I would have vitiated the one side of the Russian character that I chose as the center of my novel.

But at the time I listened to the remonstrances in silence, and fully agreed that the figure of Stolz was pale and unrealistic – not a living character but only an idea.

The Slavophiles, especially, didn't want anything to do with me, so to speak, thanks both to the unflattering character of Oblomov, and, most of all, to the German. The late F. I. Tyutchev once asked me gently, with his typical delicacy, but reprovingly, "Why did you pick Stolz?" I admitted my mistake by saying that I had done it unintentionally: "I just happened upon him!" I said.

However, it seems to me that it was beyond my control – I made no mistake if one takes into consideration the role the German element played and still plays in Russian life. They are to this day our teachers, professors, mechanics, engineers, technical experts in all areas. The best and most profitable branches of industry, trade, and other enterprises are in their hands.

This of course is troublesome, but it is just – and the reasons for such a state of affairs all stem from that selfsame *Oblomovitis* (from serfdom, among other things), whose main features I outlined in "Oblomov's Dream."

But I see it was not by chance that I happened upon a German. At the time (I've forgotten now) I must have been averse to the idea of using a pure German. So I took a Russified German, born in Russia but brought up without coddling, in the bracing and practical German manner.

Russified Germans (for example, the Ostsee people) are blending into Russian life, and though it is a slow and difficult process, no doubt they will someday blend in completely. To deny the benefits of the influx of this outside element into Russian life is both unjust and impossible. They bring to all manner of endeavors first and foremost their patience, the perseverance of their race, and many other qualities as well. And wherever it may be – in the army or navy, in administration, in science, everywhere in short – they serve at Russia's side, they serve Russia, and, for the most part, they become her children.

To rebuff them under these circumstances as a minor tributary flowing into the larger river would be just as outrageously unjust on the part of us Russians as it is outrageously unjust on the part of some Ostsee Germans who, while living in Russia, with Russians, and finding here a stable foothold for their politics and all the conditions necessary for well-being, consider Russia to be foreign to their German spirit, and back away from blending with her in an effort to maintain the status quo.

All this, of course, will change in the future, though perhaps not in the near future. The hardened stubbornness of our homegrown Germans will give in to the spirit of time when they, and their imaginary Ostsee civilization, find themselves behind a Russia marching ahead. And as Slavophilism will continue to be what it is – the expression and protection of an innate Slavic and Russian spirit, of the moral strength of the people, and the historical destiny of Russia – it will reach out in earnest to a common, i. e., European, culture. For although feelings and convictions are bound by nations, knowledge is universal.

Autobiographies

1858

In response to the request of the editorial board at *Art Page*, I have assembled and put to paper, in random fashion, some biographical information I was able to recall about myself. I am passing over in silence certain details of my childhood and youth which I intend to use in one of my future compositions – if it is meant to be.

Ivan Aleksandrovich Goncharov was born in 1813 or 1814, I do not recall the exact year,[1] in Simbirsk Province. He received his primary education, in the sciences and the French and German languages, in a small boarding school on Princess Khovanskaia's estate across the Volga, which was headed by the village priest, an intelligent and learned man married to a foreign woman. There, the first books Goncharov came across outside the classroom were the works of Derzhavin, which he copied out and memorized, then Fonvizin's *Adolescent* (they wouldn't let him read *The Brigadier*), and Ozerov and Kheraskov (he couldn't get through the latter even then, despite his childish lack of discrimination). In addition, there were several children's books on natural history, and, finally, the accounts of Kuka's travels around the world and of Krashennikov's voyage to Kamchatka. On finding them in the servants' quarters of his house, he also read the tales of Eruslan Lazarevich, Bova Koralevich, and others. And so his reading continued unsystematically and with no guidance. Most of all he devoured novels . . . travel narratives and depictions of extraordinary events – whatever seized his imagination most.

This continued until 1831, when Goncharov enrolled in the Department of Letters at Moscow University. Here his introduction to the Greek and Roman worlds, as well as the historical and critical study of Russian and foreign literatures, both instilled in him a passion for reading and provided the necessary guidance. His youthful heart sought out writers sympathetic to it, and at the time belonged to Karamzin and every new thing he came out with – not to Karamzin the historian, especially since he was all the rage in the history department, and not to Karamzin the poet, for he was no artist – but to Karamzin as the most humane of writers. At that time the founding of the new departments of aesthetics, archeology (Professor Nadezhdin), and foreign, ancient, and modern literary history (Shevirev), and the fascinating reading assigned in them, not only expanded young students' literary and aesthetic horizons but also developed their writing; that is, the necessity of taking notes at the lectures, which were given in proper and elegant Russian, naturally had a favorable effect on students' use of the language. In the meantime, independent of critical analysis in the different university departments of the ancient and modern poets and historians – students covered everything from Indian epics and dramatic tales to sacred poetry to Homer, Virgil, Tacitus, Dante, Cervantes, Shakespeare, et al. – his reading continued unabated. Goncharov was fascinated by Tasso and his *Jerusalem* for a long time, then went through a series of other writers, among whom were Klopstock and Ossian, and methodically reviewed our Russian epic writers, ending with the latest Walter Scott epic, which he studied intensively. Travel narratives and any work on natural history written in accessible language – that is, without scientific jargon – were of interest to him. But his favorite reading was poetry.

Of all the poets Goncharov read, he was most deeply affected and enamored with the poetry of Pushkin. This was at the point in the great poet's development when his powers of expression were at their freshest and most brilliant. Goncharov always remained faithful in his reverence for Pushkin, despite his later intimate knowledge of the masters of French, German, and English literature.

On completing his course work at the university, in 1835 Goncharov came to Petersburg and, following the common example, entered the civil service. He was appointed as a translator in the Ministry of Finance, and later as the head of his department, where he remained until 1852. In that year, responding to an offer made by former Minister of Education A. S. Norov, he volunteered to participate in an expedition geared toward the establishment of trade relations with Japan, was assigned by the highest authorities to the post of secretary to the head of the expedition, Vice Admiral (currently Admiral and Count) Y. V. Putiatin, and put out to sea on the frigate *Pallas*. He returned in early 1855, first assuming his prior employment, but soon thereafter was transferred to the Ministry of Education in the capacity of censor.

When not working, he devoted all his time to literature. Goncharov translated a good deal of Schiller and the prose of Goethe, as well as Winckelmann and excerpts from several English novelists; he later destroyed these translations. He had become close to the family of the painter N. A. Maikov (the father of the famous poet), and participated in their "in-house," so to speak – that is, not public – literary discussions. Later this participation moved, albeit slowly and inconspicuously, into those journals for which several friends of the Maikovs wrote. Thus Goncharov translated and edited a few foreign articles on various topics and published them unsigned in these journals. In this domestic setting he also wrote stories on similarly domestic topics, that is, stories having to do with certain private affairs or individuals, which were predominantly humorous in content and in no way remarkable.

In 1845 and 1846 he wrote the novel *A Common Story*, which was published in the February and March 1847 issues of *The Contemporary*. In 1848 he conceived the outline for the large novel *Oblomov*, wrote the first part in 1849, and published a chapter ("Oblomov's Dream") in one of the anthologies put out by *The Contemporary* that same year. In the meantime he had also written a humorous essay about the ways of petty officialdom (this was in vogue at the time) entitled "Ivan Savich Podzhabrin," which came out in the January 1848 issue of *The Contemporary*. The continuation of the novel was put off until a more opportune moment. On returning from his travels to Japan, Goncharov published, over three years, almost all the chapters of his travel log in various journals: *Sea Anthology*, *National Annals*, *The Contemporary*, *Reader's Library*, and *The Russian Herald*. This year the Moscow bookseller Glazunov gathered them together (including a new chapter on Hong Kong) and published them in two volumes under the title *The Frigate Pallas*.

In 1857 Goncharov traveled abroad, to the Marienbad springs, in order to recover from the consequences of hard work and a sedentary lifestyle. There he continued to work on *Oblomov*, which he completed in this year. The novel is currently being published in *National Annals* and is scheduled to conclude in the April issue.

1867

Born in Simbirsk in 1812, received his primary childhood education in small, private boarding schools, one of which was run by a priest across the Volga in a village on an estate. Here, under the tutelage of the priest's wife, a German who had converted to Orthodoxy, he laid the groundwork for his study of German and French. And when he found in the priest's library the books of Lomonosov and Derzhavin and others, as well as some travel narratives, the former sparked in him a passion for reading, and the latter a desire – at that time of course vague and unconscious – to see the faraway lands described in them. Before enrolling in Moscow University, he had practically no guidance in his reading. Thus he read everything he could lay his hands on – among others, works by the French writers of the dominant school of the time – and translated into Russian the novel *Atar Gull*, an excerpt of which was published in the journal *The Telescope* in 1832. But he soon sobered up from the influence of contemporary French literature, both by reading examples of English and German literature and by becoming acquainted with the ancient historians and poets while in the Department of Letters at the University. He listened hungrily to engrossing lectures on the history of foreign literatures and the fine arts, and on archeology (read by Professors Shevirev and Nadezhdin); on ancient Rome and Greece (Professors Snegirev and Ivashkovsky); on world and Russian history (Professors Kachenovsky and Pogodin); and on Russian philology (Professor Davydov). He continued to study modern languages, among them English, as well as the ancient languages Latin and, to a certain extent, Greek. Using the lectures of the learned and talented professors as his guide, Goncharov systematically studied and analyzed the exemplary works of foreign and Russian writers. At the same time, on the other hand, the strong, direct influence of Karamzin and Pushkin, who were then at the peak of their fame, on society could only have a salutary effect on the circle of young students at Moscow University – including Goncharov.

On completion of his studies, in 1835 Goncharov entered the civil service in Petersburg. He soon assumed the post of foreign correspondence translator in the Ministry of Finance, and continued to study literature – that is, he read and translated, and wrote critical abstracts, chiefly of German and English writers, as an exercise for his own benefit. He had no intention of publishing these at the time.

He became close to several families who loved literature, and he tried his hand at writing for in-house publications consisting of pieces written by a small circle of friends. All the literary talent of the time was concentrated in two magazines: *Reader's Library* and *National Annals*. Goncharov met some men of letters, at first simply as a follower; later, however, he gave his first novel, *A Common Story*, to Belinsky to judge. The novel was printed in *The Contemporary*, which had been revived after Pushkin's death, with Panaev and Nekrasov as editors, in 1847. The following year he published in the same journal the humorous sketch "Ivan Savich Podzhabrin." In 1849 an excerpt from the novel *Oblomov*, entitled "Oblomov's Dream," was printed in a collection of literary works published by *The Contemporary*.

In 1852 the then minister of education unexpectedly offered Goncharov the post of secretary to the commander of a government expedition geared toward observing the Russian colonies in North America and signing a trade agreement with Japan. He accepted the offer gladly, which suddenly awakened his cherished – and nearly abandoned – dream of traveling to distant places. On his return, after two and a half years crossing oceans and traveling from the Sea of Okhotsk through Siberia, Goncharov published in 1855 and 1856 his recollections of these travels, which appeared in segments in various journals: *Sea Anthology*, *The Contemporary*, *National Annals*, and *The Russian Herald*. In 1857 he published a separate two-volume book entitled *The Frigate Pallas*, which was reissued in a second edition of six thousand copies in 1862.

Meanwhile, in 1856 he transferred to the Ministry of Education in the capacity of censor, a job that left him almost no time for any other activities. Hard work and the Petersburg climate had a damaging effect on his health and forced him to seek mineral water treatment. During his four-month-long holiday abroad he was able to finish the novel *Oblomov*, which he had begun long before, and which finally appeared in *National Annals* in 1859. It was published as a separate book that same year, and later, in 1862, a second edition was printed.

In 1862 Goncharov was appointed editor-in-chief of the *Northern*

Post, the newspaper of the Ministry of Internal Affairs, and the following year became a member of the Ministry Publications Council. After *Oblomov*, he published three excerpts from the unfinished novel *Raisky* [i. e., *The Precipice*] – in *National Annals* and *The Contemporary* – entitled "Sofya Nikolaevna Belovodova," "The Portrait," and "Grandmother."

1874

I. A. Goncharov was born in 1814 in Simbirsk. He first studied at home, then at a boarding school where there was a small library at his disposal. This consisted of a hodgepodge of travel narratives . . . the historical works . . . the poetry . . . children's books. . . . In short, it was an unimaginable melange that he read diligently, memorizing almost everything.

This wholesale, uncritical reading, done without the slightest direction or guidance – and thus, of course, in no logical sequence – opened the boy's eyes to many things at an early age, and could only result in the accelerated development of his imagination, which was naturally overactive as it was. All this went on uncontrolled until he entered the university in 1831. Here he encountered Lermontov (during his first year, after which the poet left for Petersburg), then Stankevich and his circle – though Goncharov was in fact not acquainted with them, as he would sit at the opposite end of an immense lecture hall. Belinsky and Herzen had already left by this time. Yes, his indiscriminate reading went on until he enrolled in the Department of Philology at Moscow University in 1831; the then new professors Shevirev, Nadezhdin, and Davydov had a great impact on students – Davydov with his lectures on the history of Russian literature, Nadezhdin on the theory of fine arts and archeology, and Shevirev on the history of ancient and Western literatures. Also, in addition to teaching their courses, Davydov and Nadezhdin were writing a study of the history of general and aesthetic philosophy (the latter was Nadezhdin's specialty). Thanks to their novelty, boldness of ideas, and language, these lectures were very beneficial to the students: they brought science and art closer to life, broke out of the traditional groove by doing away with dry scholasticism, and invigorated the minds of their audience. They introduced a sober, critical approach to literature, and also had the other worthy effect of promoting the ideals of kindness, truth, beauty, perfection, progress, and so on. This all coincided with a critical turnaround in contemporary literature after its stagnation during the period of old school rhetoric, which was brought about by Pushkin and his pleiad, and by the same Nadezhdin, Polevoy, and others in the journalistic sphere.

These happy circumstances influenced many people who were fated to become important figures in their turn: Lermontov, Belinsky, K. Aksakov, Herzen, Stankevich, and others.

Upon graduation in 1834, Goncharov spent a few months at home; then, in 1835, he arrived in Petersburg and entered the civil service. He continued to devote all his free time to both Russian and foreign literature. He supplemented his education by reading everything written in Russian, German, French, and English, translated, sometimes even wrote his own work. Finally, in 1845 and 1846, he wrote a novel in two volumes entitled *A Common Story*. He had sent the first volume to Belinsky for the latter's opinion before finishing the second.

This novel was published in 1847 in *The Contemporary*, and "Oblomov's Dream" came out in that journal's *Illustrated Anthology* in 1848 (or 1849).[2] In 1852 Goncharov set off around the world as a secretary to Admiral Putiatin's mission to conclude a trade agreement with Japan. After returning, he published first excerpts of his travels in various journals, and later an account of the entire voyage in two volumes entitled *The Frigate Pallas* (1856 or 1857).[3]

In 1857, having no time in Petersburg because of his work, Goncharov went abroad to take the waters and finished *Oblomov*, of which only the first part had been completed. *Oblomov* was printed in its entirety in *National Annals* (1858 or 1859).[4]

He then began work toward the completion of the large novel *The Precipice*, which he had conceived back in 1849 and from which other pursuits and the demands of Petersburg life had torn him away. He wrote in bits and pieces, chapter by chapter, would put the novel aside for long periods, then return to it again. Finally, in 1868, he finished it hurriedly and had it published in 1868 or 1869 in *The Herald of Europe*, and then, in 1870, as a separate volume. In addition, before this (in 1848?)[5] he had published, in *The Contemporary*, a sketch on Petersburg ways entitled "Ivan Savich Podzhabrin." In 1870 he published a critical essay in *The Herald of Europe* on Griboedov's *Woe from Wit*, which he titled "The Thousand Torments."

NOTES

1. Goncharov, as becomes obvious in his autobiographies, and, in particular, in the last one, liked to be imprecise with dates. He is obviously being coy here when he pretends that he does not remember the year of his birth (1812). He assigned the same trait to Petr Aduev in *A Common Story* who is said to be vague about his age "not because of petty vanity, but owing to well thought through calculations, as if he wished to insure his life for as much as possible."

2. 1849. Goncharov, who, as his 1882 letter to A. F. Koni reprinted here testifies, remembered all kinds of dates even in his old age (including the date his insignificant translation of *Atar Gull* was published), is probably appearing uncertain about the dates of publication in order to downplay their importance to him. He was always afraid people might think he took himself too seriously.

3. 1857.

4. 1859.

5. It *was* published in 1848.

IV ❄ SELECT BIBLIOGRAPHY

Select Bibliography

Oblomov

IN RUSSIAN

Oblomov: "Literaturnye pamiatniki" Akademii Nauk SSSR (Oblomov: Literary monuments of the Academy of Sciences of the USSR). Edited by L. S. Geiro. Leningrad: Nauka, 1987.

By far the best Russian edition of *Oblomov*. The text of the novel is followed here by several manuscript variants and by Geiro's exhaustive study on the novel's history. Equally valuable are her "Notes to the Text" at the end.

Other useful editions of the novel with explanatory materials and notes include:

Polnoe sobranie sochinenii. St. Petersburg: Izdanie Glazunova, 1884. Volumes 2–3.

The only edition of complete works published during Goncharov's lifetime.

Polnoe sobranie sochinenii. St. Petersburg: Izdanie A. F. Marksa, 1899. Volumes 5–7.

Polnoe sobranie sochinenii. St. Petersburg: Izdanie Glazunova, 1912. Volumes 4–5.

Sobranie sochinenii. Moscow: Pravda, 1952. Volume 2.

Sobranie sochinenii. Moscow: Khudozhestvennaia literatura, 1953; 1979. Volume 4.

IN ENGLISH

Oblomov. Translated by C. J. Hogarth. London: Allen and Unwin, 1915.

The earliest English translation of the novel. (Constance Garnett translated Goncharov's *A Common Story* in 1894 but, for some reason, ignored *Oblomov*). Sounds very British and contains inaccuracies. Was recently republished by Bentley (Cambridge, Mass., 1979).

Oblomov. Translated by Natalie A. Duddington. New York: Macmillan, 1929.

Another relatively early English translation of *Oblomov*. Largely serviceable, but it does not do full justice to the linguistic liveliness of the original. There are also some inaccuracies. Was republished by Dutton (New York, 1953).

Oblomov. Translated by David Magarshack. London: Penguin, 1954; 1967; 1978; 1980; 1981; 1983, 1986.

The most frequently reprinted and thus commonly used translation of the novel. Quite dependable and, for the most part, accurate, with a British tint to its English. Earlier Penguin editions used, inexplicably so, Chagall's green-faced "Violinist" on their cover. Later editions have a more appropriate picture of a Russian aristocrat (much slimmer than Oblomov) at breakfast (by P. A. Fedotov).

Oblomov. Translated by Ann Dunnigan. New York: Signet, 1963.

One of the newer translations of the novel, it is competent, relatively accurate, and uses American, rather than British, idioms.

Biographies of Goncharov

Liatsky, E. A. *Goncharov: zhizn', lichnost', tvorchestvo*. Stockholm: Severnye ogni, 1920.

————. *Roman i zhizn': razvitie tvorcheskoi lichnosti Goncharova*. Prague: Plamia, 1925.

One of the strongest champions of Goncharov's talent, Liatsky in his books gives numerous biographical details based on the materials available at the time. Somewhat excessive in its insistence on the autobiographical nature of all Goncharov works, the books are nevertheless an important "corrective" to the view generally held of Goncharov at the time as a purely "impersonal" and "objective" writer.

Lilin, V. *Ivan Aleksandrovich Goncharov: Biografiia pisatelia*. Leningrad: Prosveshchenie, 1968.

A very short biography of the writer for use in Soviet schools. Both simplistic and tendentious.

Loshchits, Iury. *Goncharov*. Moscow: Molodaia gvardiia, 1977.

The biography appeared in the Soviet series *Zhizn' zamechatel'nykh liudei* (Lives of remarkable people) which practiced the odd genre of highly speculative "fictionalized" biographies where a reader is bestowed with, among other things, the subjects' inner thoughts. Has its interesting moments but is hardly reliable as a biography.

Mazon, André. *Un maître du roman russe: Ivan Gontcharov*. Paris: H. Champion, 1914.

One of the earliest biographies of Goncharov by a famous French slavist. Four years earlier Mazon also published a detailed description of the Goncharov-Turgenev literary "squabble" – "Les relations littéraires de deux maîtres du roman russe Ivan Tourguénev et Ivan Gontcharov" (*Revue de l'enseignement des langues vivantes* [November 1910]: 608–14).

Rybasov, A. *I. A. Goncharov*. Moscow: Molodaia gvardiia, 1957.

A Soviet biography of Goncharov that is factually useful but is too politically tendentious to be reliable.

Tseitlin, A. G. *I. A. Goncharov*. Moscow: AN SSSR, 1950.

Written during the last years of Stalinism, Tseitlin's biography cites Lenin and Marx more often than it cites anyone else. The only truly useful part of this biography are the endnotes that quote from some of the unpublished letters and other materials found in Goncharov archives.

Other Books, Monographs, and Articles on Goncharov and *Oblomov*

Aikhenvald, Yuly. *Siluety russkikh pisatelei*. Moscow: Nauchnoe slovo, 1906.

Aikhenvald is one of the most apt and sensitive critics of Goncharov.

Alekseev, A. D. *Letopis' zhizni i tvorchestva I. A. Goncharova*. Moscow: AN SSSR, 1960.

Like everything else that Anatoly Alekseev (1922–1990) compiled or edited on Goncharov, this is a true gem in terms of information and factual accuracy.

———. *Bibliografiia I. A. Goncharova*. Leningrad: Nauka: 1968.

———., ed. *I. A. Goncharov v portretakh, illustratsiiakh, dokumentakh*. Leningrad: Gosudarstvennoe uchebno-pedagogicheskoe izdatel'stvo, 1960.

Baratoff, Natalie. *Oblomov: A Jungian Approach. A Literary Image of the Mother Complex*. New York: Peter Lang, 1990.

Beisov, P. S. *Goncharov i rodnoi krai*. Kuibyshev: Kuibyshevskoe knizhnoe izdatel'stvo, 1960.

Blot, Jean. *Ivan Gontcharov: Ou le Réalisme Impossible*. Paris: L'Age D'Homme, 1986.

Borowec, Christine. "Time after Time: The Temporal Ideology of *Oblomov*," *Slavic and East European Journal* 4 (Winter 1994).

Chemena, O. M. *Sozdanie dvukh romanov. Goncharov i shestidesiatnitsa E. P. Maikova*. Moscow: Nauka, 1966.

Diment, Galya. *The Autobiographical Novel of Co-consciousness: Goncharov, Woolf, and Joyce*. Gainesville: University Press of Florida, 1994.

Ehre, Milton. *Oblomov and His Creator*. Princeton, N.J.: Princeton University Press, 1973.

   An excellent – and still the most definitive – English study of Goncharov and his works.

Engelgart, B. M, ed. *I. A. Goncharov i I. S. Turgenev: Po neizdannym materialam Pushkinskogo Doma*. Peterburg: Academia, 1923.

Evgen'ev-Maksimov, V. E. *I. A. Goncharov: zhizn', lichnost', tvorchestvo*. Moscow: Gosizdat, 1925.

Harper, Kenneth E. "Under the Influence of Oblomov." In *From Los Angeles to Kiev: Papers on the Occasion of the Ninth International Congress of Slavists, Kiev, September, 1983*, ed. Vladimir Markov and Dean S. Worth. Columbus: Slavica, 1983.

Huwyler-Van der Haegen, Annette. *Gončarovs drei Romane – eine Trilogie?* Munich: Otto Sagner, 1991.

Kantor, V. "Dolgii navyk k snu: Razmyshleniia o romane I. A. Goncharova *Oblomov*." *Voprosy literatury* 1 (January 1989).

Krasnoshchekova, E. A. *"Oblomov" I. A. Goncharova*. Moscow: Khudozhesvennaia literatura, 1970.

Labriolle, Francois de. "Oblomov n'est-il qu'un paresseux?" *Cahiers du monde russe et sovietique* 10.1 (1969).

Lavrin, Janko. *Goncharov: Studies in Modern European Literature and Thought*. New Haven: Yale University Press, 1954.

Lohff, Ulrich M. *Die Bildlichkeit in den Romanen Ivan Aleksandrovic Goncarovs*. Munich: Otto Sagner, 1977.

Louria, Yvette, and Morton I. Seiden. "Ivan Goncharov's *Oblomov*: The Anti-Faust as Christian Hero." *Canadian Slavic Studies*, 3, no. 1 (1969).

Lyngstad, Alexandra, and Sverre Lyngstad. *Ivan Goncharov*. New York: Twayne, 1971.

   Has the limitations of all volumes in the "Twayne's World Authors" series insofar as it is too brief and too general but, overall, a sensitive and sensible study of Goncharov's major works.

Matlaw, Ralph E, ed. *Belinsky, Chernyshevsky, and Dobrolyubov: Selected Criticism*. Bloomington: Indiana University Press, 1976.

Contains an English translation of Dobrolyubov's "What is Oblomovitis?"

Mays, Milton A. "Oblomov as Anti-Faust." *Western Humanities Review* 21 (1967).

Merezhkovsky, D. *Vechnye sputniki: Dostoevsky, Goncharov, Maikov.* St. Petersburg: Izdanie M. V. Pirozhkova, 1908.

Molinari, Sergio. *Razionalità ed Emozione: Osservazioni sullo stile di Ivan Goncarov.* Padova, Italy: Marsilio Editori, 1970.

Otradin, M. V., ed. *Roman I. A. Goncharova "Oblomov" v russkoi kritike.* Leningrad: Izdatel'stvo Leningradskogo universiteta, 1991.

Peace, Richard. *Oblomov: A Critical Examination of Goncharov's Novel* Birmingham, England: University of Birmingham, 1991.

Piksanov, N. K., ed. *Goncharov v vospominaniiakh sovremennikov.* Leningrad: Khudozhestvennaia literatura, 1969.

Poggioli, Renato. *The Phoenix and the Spider.* Cambridge: Harvard University Press, 1957.

Pokrovsky, V. I., ed. *Ivan Goncharov: ego zhizn' i sochineniia.* Moscow: Magazin V. Spiridonova i A. Mikhailova, 1912.

Poliakov, M. Ia., and S. A. Trubnikov, eds. *I. A. Goncharov v russkoi kritike.* Moscow: Khudozhestvennaia literatura, 1958.

Pritchett, V. S. "An Irish Oblomov." In *The Working Novelist.* London: Chatto and Windus, 1965.

Prutskov, N. I. *Masterstvo Goncharova romanista.* Moscow: AN SSSR, 1962.

Russell, Mechtild. *Untersuchungen zur Theorie und Praxis der Typisierung bei I. A. Goncarov.* Munich: Otto Sagner, 1978.

Rybasov, A. P., ed. *I. A. Goncharov. Literaturno-kriticheskie stat'i i pis'ma.* Leningrad: Khudozhestvennaia literatura, 1938.

Setchkarev, Vsevolod. *Ivan Goncharov: His Life and His Works.* Wurzburg: Jal, 1974.

Stilman, Leon. "Oblomovka Revisited." *The American Slavic and East European Review* 7 (1948).

Still one of the very best articles written on Goncharov in English.

Terry, Garth M. *Ivan Goncharov: A Bibliography.* Nottingham, England: Astra Press, 1986.

A very useful bibliography in English that includes dissertations and works published in Russia, the Soviet Union, the United States, and Europe.

Thiergen, Peter, ed. *I. A. Goncarov: Beiträge zu Werk und Wirkung.* Köln: Böhlau, 1989.

————. *Ivan A. Goncarov. Leben, Werk und Wirkung. Beiträge der I. Internationalen Goncarov-Konferenz Bamberg, 8–10 Oktober 1991.* Köln: Böhlau Verlag, 1994.
An excellent recent collection of papers and articles in German, Russian, and English.

Wigzell, Faith. "Dream and Fantasy in Goncharov's *Oblomov*." In *From Pushkin to Palisandriia: Essays on the Russian Novel in Honor of Richard Freeborn.* Edited by Arnold McMillin. New York: St. Martin's Press, 1990.

Zakharkin, A. F. *Roman I. A. Goncharova "Oblomov".* Moscow: Uchpedgiz, 1963.